~The Compl[e]
for Parents with
DISABLED
CHILDREN

John A. Sterba, M.D., Ph.D.
and Janice E. Sterba

PRESS

ACW Press
Phoenix, Arizona 85013

Preface

"Shouldn't there be a handbook for parents like us,
to help us find everything we need to know?"

As parents of a child with disabilities, we searched for information to help us from various sources, including:

- Prayer.
- Advice from many doctors, therapists and teachers.
- Advice from family members.
- Personal experience from other families with children having disabilities.
- Our own trials and errors.
- Local, state and federal organizations, resources and publications.
- Medical literature searches.
- Articles from medical journals and many magazines.
- The few books written to help parents like us.
- Internet searches.
- State and federal laws
- Legal advice on the rights of children with disabilities.

We designed this handbook to be easy-to-use. Small enough for the glove compartment or diaper bag, the handbook will be very useful in the doctor's office, at the therapist, or even during yearly planning meeting with the Committee on Special Education (CSE) for your child's Individualized Educational Program (IEP).

We have compiled a lot of accurate information plus many support services and professionals to help care for a child with a disability. We incorporated our two file cabinets of information into this handbook plus extensive searches for relevant information. Since we continue to learn, especially networking with other families of children with disabilities, we have provided you with a questionnaire at the end of the handbook. Please contribute to help other families for future editions of this handbook. Share information about a service you offer, changes and corrections, or suggestions from what you have learned from your own family experiences.

The main purpose of this handbook is to give you hope and information. We have faith that it will help you and your children. The handbook will also help you by taking away some stress from your busy family life. We hope that this valuable information will prepare you for each step you must take in raising a child with a disability.

John and Janice Sterba
March 3, 2002

Contents

<u>Appendices</u>

<u>Questionnaire:</u>

Introduction

The purpose of this handbook is to help you as a parent of a child with a disability to easily find useful information as well as federal, state and local resources. We hope the handbook will also help you to discover your child's dreams, interests and hidden potentials.

As parents, we all try to encourage our children's independence, self-esteem and happiness. The handbook has many chapters and sections on receiving help through prayer, special educational services, assistive technology devices and services, assistance programs and information centers, sports therapy and recreational programs for the rehabilitation and overall well-being of your child.

The handbook will also give you practical guidelines for becoming a more effective advocate for your child when speaking with your child's teachers, school board administrators and therapists to ensure your child receives the "most appropriate and least restrictive" services. State and U.S. federal laws are referenced and summarized to empower you to legally acquire school-supported services. As legally required by the United States Department of Education, parents of disabled children must receive the Due Process Rights for Parents of Children with Disabilities, which is included to clearly outline all your rights.

Personal family issues are also reviewed, including respite, developing your child's independence, looking out for your child's safety, counseling for families facing challenges, home and car modifications for better accessibility, vacation and travel tips, and inside tips for maximizing medical insurance reimbursement.

We have included a section with medical diagnoses and disabilities explained in layperson's terms. This will help you to work more closely with all your child's doctors, healthcare providers, and therapists to meet your child's many needs.

The handbook should not be used to contradict any information, advice or recommendations that you receive from your child's physicians, therapists, healthcare providers or teachers. The handbook also does not recommend or promote one service, agency or healthcare provider over another.

We strongly encourage others to share their current information or suggestions with us for consideration in a future edition of the handbook. Please complete and mail in the questionnaire on the last page. This way you can share with other families what services you offer or what you have learned as a parent, therapist or healthcare provider. This networking between parents and sharing of information is a most effective way of helping each other with useful, highly recommended information.

Prayer

This is my testimony as a father. After my daughter was born and I later learned how serious the medical situation had become for her, I was immediately overwhelmed. I experienced fear, sadness, isolation and nauseating grief with a severe sense of hopelessness. Do you know these feelings? Despite ongoing excellent medical advice and the care of many doctors, I was alone. I had no place to turn except to God for help. I prayed that He would please help my daughter and to please help me get through this. I heard in my heart, *I have never left you.* While I was praying, I had a warm, embracing feeling of the presence of Jesus, right next to me.

Recently, I found the Bible verse that describes that feeling of comfort and assurance that Jesus gave me that day: *Do not be anxious about anything, but in everything, by prayer and petition, with thanksgiving, present your requests to God. And the peace of God, which transcends all understanding, will guard your hearts and your minds in Christ Jesus* (Philippians 4:4-7).

His presence has never left me, as He promised, *And surely I am with you always, to the very end of the age* (Matthew 28:20b). *The Lord himself goes before you and will be with you; He will never leave you nor forsake you. Do not be afraid; do not be discouraged* (Deuteronomy 31:8).

This is our testimony as a family. Janice and I were married in 1997. We share joint custody of my daughter. Since that time, the Lord has continued to oversee everything good that has come to help our daughter, in so many areas of physical, emotional and spiritual needs. Four years ago, our daughter was ten years old and doing very well in all areas of her life, especially her physical rehabilitation. She was truly enjoying the end of a great year in third grade. All was well, on an even keel.

On June 10, 1998 at 6:35 A.M., on a country road, while I was driving to work, I felt the Lord speak to me in my heart three times, like a command, *Help the children.* I ignored His voice in my heart. The third time He said, *Help the children.* He added, *You know what to do.* In my heart I just said, "Oh no! Everything is fine now—I've got a good full-time job, and I'm trying to pay off all the debts and everything is going great now, and…" The Lord was very patient with me while I was whining.

I then tried to bargain with the Lord: "Do you mean medical research, like rehabilitation research? I don't know much about rehabilitation research, or do you mean me medically caring for handicapped children? Lord, I do that now in the ER, every now and then, and…" I just stopped complaining. Tears came over me and I admitted to the Lord I didn't know how to "Help the children." In my prayers, I told the Lord how grateful I was for all He had done for our daughter. I prayed for Him to please show me how to "Help the children." The same peace that only comes from the Lord came into my heart, now with tears of joy.

Years before, I had asked Jesus to please forgive my sins and to please be my Lord and Savior and that I believed He died for the forgiveness of my sins as the Son of God. He saved me that day and has never left me. On that stretch of country road on my way to work in 1998, He again let me know that He had *never* left me, and I knew in my heart He would *never, ever* leave me.

When I got home that night, I told my wife, Janice, about how the Lord spoke in my heart, *"Help the children"* three times. We prayed together. As a couple, we knew we had to continue to turn to the Lord, every day. We were overwhelmed that we may not have time for more prayer, daily reading from the Bible and now "Helping the children" on top of both of us working, plus caring for our daughter and all the debt, etc.

We noticed the two file cabinets of medical rehabilitation information we had gathered while taking care of our daughter with her multiple disabilities. My wife and I then began writing this handbook for you, starting with a simple outline of everything a parent of a child with a disability needs to know. The Lord has guided our paths ever since.

Please, never stop praying. Trust in the Lord. He always provides to meet exactly what He knows we need. It wasn't how much faith we had, for we had very little back then. It was how we trusted Him as our heavenly Father to provide for all our family needs. Speak with the pastor of your church for guidance on prayer and for support. If you don't attend any church, seek the Lord by finding a church and asking the pastor for help. Recently we found the Bible verse that explains how we know that God is always in control of everything: *And we know that in all things God works for the good of those who love Him, who have been called according to His purpose* (Romans 8:28).

Our daughter's many doctors continue to be very perplexed and amazed with her remarkable progress, saying, "…Well…whatever you're doing…ah… just keep doing it." Praise God.

As a physician, I find it awesome to see the way the Lord heals. Because of Jesus Christ, He has healed the broken body and broken spirit of our daughter, and Jesus has healed many broken hearts in our families for those who have turned to Him. The Lord has also opened up so much more free time and provided people to help our daughter, plus enough financial resources. We can't explain how He does it; we are grateful to be blessed with His constant presence in our lives and hearts.

Trust in Jesus, no matter how small you think your faith is. The Lord will help you and your child, too. *What is faith? It is the confident assurance that what we hope for is going to happen. It is the evidence of things we cannot yet see. God gave his approval to people in days of old because of their faith* (Hebrews 11:1-2).

Please pray. And when you get discouraged, or scared, and even broken down with despair, *pray some more.* The Lord always hears your prayers. Jesus loves families and all children are precious to Him. The Lord fearfully and wonderfully makes all children. God is not to blame for tragedies happening to children or families, so stop blaming God if you are angry. *For you created my inmost being; you knit me together in my mother's womb. I praise you because I am fearfully and wonderfully made; your works are wonderful, I know that full well* (Psalm 139:13-14). It is all right to be angry, just don't blame God. Ask God to please take your anger away. Pray for Him to show you His way, which is always the best, and so is His timing in everything.

The Lord loves every one of us and He wants us to turn to Him for help. *For God so loved the world that He gave his one and only Son, that whoever believes in Him shall not perish but have eternal life. For God did not send His Son into the world to condemn the world, but to save the world through Him* (John 3:16-17). He can take away your sorrow, your anger, and your bitterness. Just pray and tell Him all about it and ask for help. He'll be there waiting, patiently, for you to turn to Him for help, just like a loving Father. *As the scriptures tell us, "Anyone who believes in Him will not be disappointed"* (Romans 10:11).

Start praying with your spouse. If you are alone as a single parent like I was seven years ago, then pray by yourself. *The earnest prayer of a righteous person has great power and wonderful results* (James 5:16b).

The Lord saves us through our faith in Him, not our deeds or how much we go to church or perform traditions, rituals, etc. *For it is by grace you have been saved, through faith—and this not from yourselves, it is a gift of God—not by works, so that no one can boast* (Ephesians 2:8-9). *"The word is near you; it is in your mouth and in your heart," that is, the word of faith we are proclaiming: That if you confess with your mouth, "Jesus is Lord," and believe in your heart that God raised Him from the dead, you will be saved. For it is with your heart that you believe and are justified, and it is with your mouth that you confess and are saved* (Romans 10:8–10).

Go find a quiet place and pray. The Lord already knows what you need, even before you ask Him. So keep it simple. You do have to ask, though, so go ahead and pray. Jesus Christ is much more important than any advice from a family member, friend or physician or any of the information we give to you in this handbook. Please put the handbook aside and pray.

Our prayer for you is that you turn to Jesus and that you trust in Him to provide all your needs. We pray that when you trust in Him, that you experience His comfort and assurance that He will never leave you. May this handbook be a source of encouragement and help to you and your child.

Special Education Services

- General Information on Special Education Services
- Committee on Special Education (CSE)
- Individualized Educational Program (IEP)
- Individualized Family Service Plan (IFSP)
- Homeschooling
- Least Restrictive School Setting
- Mainstreaming
- Related Services
- Transition Services

General Information on Special Education Services

Special Education Services, including specially designed educational instruction, supplementary devices, classroom or personal aides (teacher/student assistant) and other related services (example: physical, occupational and speech therapies, counseling, and others described in detail, below) *must be provided, at no cost* to the parents of children from ages 3 through 21 that qualify. This is *guaranteed* by U.S. federal legislation, which specifies the rights of the parents, who are to be actively involved in the educational decision-making process for their child. Parents have the legal right to work closely with the school district and to actively advocate for specific programs, services, classroom settings, and acquire assistive technology devices and services that will allow their child to benefit from their educational program. For further information, see chapter 5, Assistive Technology Devices and Services. These rights for both parents and their child are documented in the Individuals with Disabilities Education Act (IDEA) (Public Law 101-476), formerly known as the Education of Handicapped Children's Act (Public Law 94-142), and the most recent, IDEA Amendments of 1997 (Public law 105-17).

The Committee on Special Education (CSE). The CSE will make the determination that a child can receive special education services only after they evaluate and conclude that the child has a disability that interferes with a regular educational program. Such disabilities include impairments in hearing, vision, speech, or orthopedic impairment, mental retardation or learning and behavioral disabilities. The CSE usually consists of the director or assistant director of the school district's department of special education as the CSE chairperson, the school psychologist, a school administrator, the child's teacher, therapist(s) (e.g. physical, occupational or speech therapists), the child's parent(s) and another parent of a disabled child as the parent advocate. A parent may request a CSE evaluation from their local school board if that parent feels their child needs special education or related services.

The Individualized Educational Program (IEP). The CSE with direct involvement of the family must first develop a legal document called the Individualized Educational Program or IEP. The IEP identifies all the special education services that must be legally provided for the child, *at no cost to the family*, including supplementary devices, assistive technology devices and services, classroom or personal aides and other related services. The IEP documents how often the special education services must be provided, describes any specialized equipment and indicates the recommended educational program and placement. For example, **1:6:1** means 1 teacher:6 students:1 aide, and **1:12:1** means 1 teacher:12 students:1 aide. The school must evaluate a child's placement and program every year, usually in the spring anticipating summer school, if recommended by the CSE, and the next academic school year.

Following the CSE meeting, the IEP is drafted and submitted to the family. If the family disagrees with the recommendations and findings of the CSE on the IEP, the family has the legal right to request an independent evaluation. For example, by New York state law, the school district is responsible to pay for the cost of this independent evaluation.

Furthermore, the school district is required, by federal and New York state laws, to give the family a document called "Your Rights as a Parent" which is the Due Process Rights for Parents of Children with Disabilities required by the United States Department of Education. This lengthy document is provided to you following this section on Special Education Services. There may small differences between states, but we feel the New York state edition is very complete and easy to understand.

A parent may review all of their child's records and obtain copies of these records, but the school may charge a reasonable fee for photo-copying. If the school refuses a request from a parent to change the records due to the records being misleading, inaccurate or violating the rights or privacy of their child, the parent has the right to request a **hearing** to challenge this questionable information in the child's records. If the parent disagrees with the findings of the hearing, the parent may also file a complaint with the state education agency.

The specific address of your state's education agency can be found by calling your local school board, the Committee on Special Education or through your state's Web site: www.state.(then type the U.S. mail two-letter abreviation for your state, like IL for Illinois).us. For example, the state of Illinois' Web site would be www.state.IL.us. You can then search your state's Web site for specific topics on your rights and your child's rights in special education through the Department of Education, the attorney general's office or searching based on your child's specific disability. For example, in New York State, there is the **New York State Office of Advocate for Persons with Disabilities**, which can assist parents that need to file a complaint (phone: (800)-522-4369, voice/TTY with full address, e-mail and Web site, below).

A parent should be encouraged to participate in the development of the child's **Individualized Education Program (IEP)**. For children younger than three years old, the IEP equivalent is called the **Individualized Family Service Plan (IFSP)**. The IEP and IFSP are written, legal documents of the educational programs designed to meet the unique needs of the child. The school must make every effort to notify the parent of the IEP or IFSP meeting and to arrange the meeting at a time and place that is convenient for both the parent and the school. A parent may request an IEP or IFSP meeting at any time throughout the school year through their local school district.

Homeschooling. Parents that **homeschool** their children can also request an IEP through their local school district. For example, in the New York State Education Department, you can learn more on home-schooling through the elementary middle secondary and continuing education website: www.emsc.nysed.gov. Under the "Offices in EMSC" heading, click on the "Regional School and Community Services RSCS" heading. Under the "Topics" heading, click on the "Home Instructions" heading. This will bring up the "Home Instruction in New York State" information sheet. You may then choose "Click here for Home Instruction Questions and Answers" or "Click here for a Listing of Groups of Home Instructing Parents" for more current information. This information sheet also contains some pertinent facts about home instruction in New York State under Section 100.10 of the Regulations of the New York State Commissioner of Education (see http://www.emsc.nysed.gov/rscs/regulations/homeinstructionreg.html). If you have further questions about home instruction in New York State, contact the Nonpublic Schools Unit at (518) 474-3879 or by e-mail: mailto:nmoore@mail.nysed.gov.

Least Restrictive School Setting. A parent has the legal right to have their child educated in the least restrictive school setting possible. The legal term, *least restrictive*, should always be used. Don't use other terms such as "the best" or your best of intentions will be met with resistance resulting in frustration.

Mainstreaming. The school is required by federal and state laws to make every effort to develop an appropriate educational program that will provide the child with the services and supports, which are needed in order for your child to be taught with children who do not have disabilities. This is called *mainstreaming*.

Related Services. All children determined to need an IEP will be evaluated to receive appropriate related services at no cost, as documented by federal law (Individuals with Disabilities Education Act (IDEA) (Public Law 101-476) and the IDEA Amendments of 1997 (Public law 105-17), Section 300.24 of the Federal Register).

Related services are transportation, and such developmental, corrective, and other supportive services (including speech-language pathology and audiology services, psychological services, physical and occupational therapy, recreation, including therapeutic recreation, [also called sports therapy] social work services, counseling services, including rehabilitation counseling, orientation and mobility services, except that such medical services shall be for diagnostic and evaluation purposes only) as may be required to help a child with a disability to benefit from special education (Section 1401 (22), 1997 Reauthorization of IDEA).

What are these **Related Services?**

1. **Audiology.** The study of hearing disorders through the identification and measurement of hearing function loss as well as the rehabilitation of children with hearing impairments by hearing specialists called audiologists.
2. **Counseling Services.** Counseling services for your child provided by licensed providers, including psychologists, social workers and guidance counselors.
3. **Early Identification and Assessment of Disabilities in Children.** A plan to identify any disabilities as early as possible in the child's life.
4. **Medical Services.** A licensed physician, with either an M.D. (Doctor of Medicine) or D.O. (Doctor of Osteopathy), will take a medical history and conduct a physical exam to determine the medical disability diagnoses, which require special education and related services.
5. **Occupational Therapy.** Occupational therapists (OTs) provide therapy by means of various activities, for example activities of daily living (ADL), prescribed for the effect on promoting recovery or rehabilitation.
6. **Orientation and Mobility Services.** These are services to visually challenged or blind students by qualified providers to enable safe movement in the school, home and community.
7. **Parent Counseling and Training.** Education and counseling services are available to parents to help them understand their child's disabilities and many needs, plus methods of providing care and coping in the home.
8. **Physical Therapy.** Physical therapists (PTs) provide therapy by physical and mechanical means, for example massage and

joint manipulation, regulated exercise, thermal and electrical stimulation.

9. **Psychological Services.** Licensed psychologists conduct a clinical psychological and behavioral assessment and develop a school and home-based program for the parents and the child, which includes positive behavioral modifications.

10. **Recreation.** The recreation assessment includes adapted physical education (APE) evaluation. Adapted physical education provides a modification and/or adaptation of various physical education activities to meet the individual needs of the student. The adapted physical education program may be designed for individual or group activities. Activities included in this program are physical fitness skills, movement and rhythmic skills, playground and life-time sports skills, and aquatic skills. Related services can include the adapted physical education requirements during school as well as recreation and leisure programs after school, at home and in the community. Also see chapter 11, Sports Therapy; chapter 12, Recreational Programs and chapter 13, Directory of Sports Therapy and Recreational Programs in the U.S and Canada.

11. **Rehabilitation Counseling Services.** These are services focusing on developing confidence and independence, employment preparation, career development and integration into the community and workplace.

12. **School Health Services.** These are healthcare services provided by a licensed healthcare provider such as a school nurse.

13. **Social Worker Services in School.** The social worker provides individual and/or group counseling sessions in school, updates the social and developmental history on the child, works with the teachers and the parents on school, home and community issues, makes available both school and community resources to encourage learning and independent behavior, determines eligibility for Supplemental Security Income (SSI), and encourages transition services, see below.

14. **Speech Therapy.** Also known as language pathology services, speech therapy identifies speech and language impairments, sets up referrals for medical and/or speech pathologist evaluations, and treats the speech impairments, helping to prevent further communication impairments.

15. **Transportation.** Transportation includes not only bussing to and from school and in the community during school-planned activities, but also safety issues, mobility issues of lifts and aids aboard the bus, mobility issues in and around the school, and any specialized equipment that may be needed.

Transition Services. The federal law (Individuals with Disabilities Education Act (IDEA), defines transition services as a coordinated set of activities for a student designed within an outcome-oriented process, that promotes movement from post-school activities including post-secondary education, vocational training, integrated employment, and continuing and adult education, adult services, independent living, or community participation; and is based on the individual student's needs, taking into account the student's preferences and interests. The activity areas include instruction, community experience, related services, development of employment and other post-school adult living objectives; and if appropriate, acquisition of daily living skills and functional vocational evaluation (Section 1401 (30) of the 1997 Reauthorization of IDEA).

Components of a Comprehensive Special Education Evaluation

TYPE OF EVALUATION	TO OBTAIN INFORMATION ABOUT:	OFTEN CONDUCTED BY:
Physical examination	Sight, hearing, physical development, medical needs, physical and health factors that affect school progress	School physician
Individual psychological evaluation	General intelligence, learning strengths and weaknesses, instructional needs, social interactions and relationships	School psychologist
Social history	Social development, current social interactions, factors with the home, school and community that may contribute to student's difficulties	School social worker, school nurse, counselor, school psychologist
Classroom observation	Performance in the current educational setting, relationship to teachers and other students, learning styles, attention span	School administrator, reading specialist, guidance counselor, committee on special education (CSE) member, school psychologist

Appropriate educational evaluations	Educational achievement, learning strengths and weaknesses, vocational and academic needs	Teachers, reading specialist, guidance counselor, educational evaluators, vocational counselors, school psychologist
Assessments on all areas relating to the suspected disability	A specific disability related to health, vision, hearing, social-emotional development, general intelligence, communication skills, motor abilities and academic performance	Private medical doctor, school nurse, ophthalmologist, audiologist, speech pathologist, speech therapist, physical and occupational therapists, teacher, behavioral specialist or other specialist with knowledge in the area of suspected disability

Becoming the Most Effective
Parent Advocate for Your Child

To become the *most effective parent advocate* for your child, each parent must not only understand their own legal rights but also become actively involved to protect their child's rights and what they are entitled to by federal law. An excellent source of information is the **Educational Resource Information Center (ERIC)**. As explained in the ERIC Web site, (www.ed.gov/EdRes/EdFed/ERIC.html), the mission of the ERIC system includes improving American education by increasing and facilitating the use of educational research and information to improve practice in learning, teaching, educational decision-making, and research, wherever and whenever these activities take place. ERIC also serves the needs of teachers, professors, and librarians; school and college administrators, counselors, instructional media staff, and support personnel; educational researchers; educational policymakers at every level; students and non-formal learners at every age and level, including adult learners; parents; health and social services personnel and caregivers who support families, parents, students, and children; and the media and business communities as they relate to education. In 1996, the ERIC system established goals to provide easy, affordable access to ERIC bibliographic and full-text resources from every school, library, household, and point of educational decision making; expand ERIC's database and services to make useful information available to all categories of users; expand the ERIC information-synthesizing function to include a greater number and variety of publications and to use a greater variety of dissemination methods; deliver documents in various full-text electronic formats as well as in microfiche and paper forms; and further develop electronic access to ERIC, including the development of virtual libraries and Web sites.

The **Educational Resource Information Center (ERIC)** can be reached by calling (800) LET-ERIC (538-3742). The ERIC Web site is: www.ed.gov/EdRes/EdFed/ERIC.html. ERIC also offers parents many brochures that provide tips for becoming more involved in their children's education.

Below are suggestions taken in part from the 1998 U.S. Department of Education in the **ERIC Digest, "Rights and Responsibilities of Parents of Children with Disabilities"** (in italics), followed by our own experience and lessons learned.

1. *Develop a partnership with the school and share relevant information about your child's education and development.* Get to personally know your child's teachers, therapists and aides.
2. *Ask for clarification of any aspect of the program that is unclear to you.*
3. *Make sure you understand the program specified in the Individualized Education Program (IEP) or the IEP equivalent, called the Individualized Family Service Plan (IFSP) before agreeing to it or signing the form.* Take the IEP or IFSP form home so you can review it before you sign it. You have ten *school days* in which to make a decision. Review the proposed IEP or IFSP with another experienced family having a challenged or disabled child. Networking with other families of challenged or disabled children is most effective in learning about the details of the IEP or IFSP process, your rights as a parent and your child's rights.
4. *Consider and discuss with your child's teacher how your child might be included in the regular school activities program.* Do not forget areas such as lunch, recess, art, music and physical education as well as after-school programs (cheerleading, drama club, pep rallies and dances) or even before-school programs (breakfast).
5. *Monitor your child's progress and periodically ask for a report.* If your child is not progressing, discuss this with the teacher and determine whether the program should be modified. Meet with your child's teachers, therapists and aides after school or as often as your schedule allows.
6. *Discuss with the school* (e.g. aide, teacher, principal, CSE chairperson in that order) *any problems that occur with your child's assessment, placement or educational program.* If you are uncertain

about how to resolve a problem, you can turn to the advocacy agencies that are found in most states for the guidance you need to pursue your case. Each state has an office to assist those with disabilities. In your state, contact your local school board Committee on Special Education. If they cannot help, begin with your states' attorney general's office for guidance. For example, see appendix 1, Support Services and Legal Assistance, Western New York State.

7. To search your state's Web site to locate information on your child's special education needs or your advocacy rights through the attorney general's office, you can also use your state's specific Web site: www.state.(then type the U.S. mail two-letter abrevia-tion for your state, like IL for Illinois).us. For example, the state of Illinois' Web site would be www.state.IL.us.

8. *Keep records.* There may be many questions and comments about your child that you will want to discuss, as well as notes from meetings and phone conversations that you will want to remember. A spiral notebook journal is sufficient. Be thorough and take detailed notes including names/titles/phone numbers of people who promise services or follow-up on questions you have for your child. Make sure you write down your questions before you go into a meeting and make sure they all get answered.

9. *Join a parent organization.* In addition to giving parents an opportunity to share considerable knowledge, experience and gain support, a parent group can be a most effective force on behalf of your child.

10. *Direct observation in the classroom.* When selecting a new class-room or next year's new placement, visit the classroom and directly observe the teacher as well as privately meet the teacher, one-on-one. To speak with parents of children in this teacher's classroom, ask permission for their name and phone number. This is a very effective way of learning about the teacher, the school and the support from administration.

11. *Become more involved in the IEP or IFSP Process.* Know what you want your child to learn. Bring copies of all information that may be helpful to the IEP/IFSP meeting (medical records, testing results, past school records). Be prepared to discuss the most effective method you have found for disciplining your child. Ask

what you can do at home to support the program such as tutoring or home computer-assisted learning or other assistive technological devices and services.

12. *Be professional.* For your child's IEP or IFSP meeting, be prompt and dress in the best clothes you would wear to church. You will be taken seriously if you act and look professional. You are representing your child, like an attorney, at this legally required meeting that will determine an entire year of education and services for your child. Bring your list of questions or concerns, take detailed notes, and *do not allow the CSE meeting to end until you have received clear answers to all your questions.* These people on the CSE are indeed busy and dedicated. They are also required by federal law to include you in this IEP/IFSP process. Fixing a small mistake or misunderstanding can be done by the CSE at this IEP/IFSP meeting, or it may take an attorney, thousands of dollars and a lot of frustration to do it later. Before the CSE meeting, you should have privately met with your child's teacher, aide and therapists to carefully and completely go over all the issues. It is essential to settle all issues with your child's special education teacher long before the CSE IEP meeting, which is usually scheduled for 15-30 minutes, so be prepared. If you feel confused or overwhelmed, meet with another, experienced parent of a child with disabilities for one-on-one guidance before the CSE IEP meeting. This is often very helpful to get organized and to learn what questions to ask of your child's teacher or of the CSE at the IEP meeting. If you are still having trouble getting organized, ask the CSE chairperson if you could have another experienced parent of a disabled child accompany you.

Readings and Organizations for Becoming the Most Effective Parent Advocate

To become the most effective parent advocate for your child, here are some suggested readings and useful organizations:

"Parents!"

This easy to use booklet identifies techniques for the parents to prepare themselves to become an effective team member in planning their child's education program and strategies they can use to make the IEP procedures, timelines and federal and state laws work for their child. The booklet, which has useful information for all states, can be requested from:

NYS Office of Advocate for Persons with Disabilities
Technology-Related Assistance for Individuals with Disabilities
(TRAID) Project
One Empire State Plaza, Suite 1001
Albany, NY 12223-1150
Phone: (800) 522-4369 (Voice/TTY/Spanish)
E-mail: information@oapwd.state.ny.us
Web site: www.advoc4disabled.state.ny.us

"A Parent's Guide to Special Education for Children Ages 5-21: Your Child's Right to an Education in New York State."

This free guide describes the special educational services and programs and the rights for both parents and their children with challenges and disabilities to have a free, least restrictive and appropriate public education. This book is referenced by U.S. Federal Legislation, Individuals with Disabilities Education Act (IDEA), (Public Law 101-476). Part 1 discusses the special education process and Part 2 is a practical handbook with recommendations for record keeping, parent advocacy, due process and parental rights. Resource materials are listed. The booklet can be requested by anyone, not just New York State residents, from the Vocational and Educational Services for Individual with Disabilities (VESID):

New York State Education Department
VESID - Special Education Policy Unit
Room 1624 OCP
Albany, NY 12234
ATTN: "Parent's Guide", "Publications Unit"
Phone: (518) 473-2878
Web site: www.nysed.gov/vesid, click on Special Education or Publications

"Your School Records- Questions and Answers about a Set of Rights for Parents and Students:"
The Children's Defense Fund originally published this free guide to provide information about the Family Educational Rights and Privacy Act. This is also known as the Buckley Amendment. To request a free copy, write or call:

NYS Commission on Quality of Care
99 Washington Avenue, Suite 1002
Albany, New York 12210
Phone: (800) 624-4143
Web site: www.cqc.state.ny.us

"Individuals with Disabilities Education Act (IDEA), P.L. 101-467, 1990: Assistance to States for the Education of Children with Disabilities...Final Rule." Tuesday, September 29, 1993.

This is the U.S. federal law, with its regulations, and governs educational programs for children with disabilities, nationally. IDEA (P.L.101 – 407) is the reauthorization law of the original education law (P.L.94-142), which is for children with disabilities. If you would like a copy of this, call or write to your United States Congressman or Senator. Usually, single copies are free. Include the Federal Register date with the other information listed above. To get a copy of your State Education Department's memo regarding compliance with these federal regulations and excerpts of sections that discuss assistive technology, contact the *Regional Technology Related Assistance for Individuals with Disabilities (TRAID Project)*. See chapter 5 on Assistive Technology Devices and Services, below, for more information.

"Fundamentals of Assistive Technology" Third Edition, 2000.

This comprehensive resource manual, costing $50.00, contains twelve modules written by experts in the field of assistive technology, including funding and federal policies and legislation such as the Technology Related Assistance for Individuals with Disabilities Act of 1988 (Tech Act), which applies for each state from Rehabilitation Engineering and Assistive Technology Society of North America (RESNA). This manual and other valuable references and booklets are available from:

RESNA Technical Assistance Project
1700 N. Moore Street, Suite 1540
Arlington, VA 22209-1903
Phone: (703) 524-6686, Ext. 310
E-mail: info@resna.org
Web site: www.resna.org and link to Publication

Family Resource Center on Disabilities. *"How to Get Services by Being Assertive."*

This covers assertive vs. non-assertive behaviors, eliminating your negatives, developing your positives, assertiveness exercises, assertiveness with bureaucrats and public officials and assertiveness at special education meetings. Cost of this book is $12.00 ($10.00 + $2.00 postage). For a copy, call or write to:

Family Resource Center
220 S. State
Chicago, IL 60604
Phone: (312) 939-3513
Web site: www.frcd.org

Focus on the Family: Ministries, Resource Center, Syndicated International Radio Broadcasts for Children and Adults and Focus on the Family Magazine.

Taken in part from the Focus on the Family's Guiding Principles: The values and techniques taught to parents are drawn from the wisdom of the Bible and Judeo-Christian ethic, rather than from the humanistic notions of today's theorists. In short, Focus on the Family is a reflection of what we believe to be the recommendations of the Creator Himself, who ordained the family and gave it His blessing.

Focus on the Family
8605 Explorer DriveColorado Springs, CO 80995
Phone: (800) 232-6459; (TDD): (877) 877-0503 or (719) 548-4601
Fax: (719) 531-3424
Web site: www.family.org

Assistive Technology Devices and Services

- Individuals with Disabilities Education Act (IDEA)
- Computers with Software/Hardware Adaptations
- Assistive Listening Devices: Hearing Aids, FM, TV, TTY, TDD, etc.
- Classroom Modifications
- Medicaid or Private Insurance
- Section 504 of the Federal Rehabilitation Act
- United States Department of Education
- Office of Special Education and Rehabilitation Services (OSERS)
- Office of Special Education Programs (OSEP)
- Rehabilitation Services Administration (RSA)
- National Institute on Disability and Rehabilitation Research (NIDRR)
- Regional Technology Related Assistance for Individuals with Disabilities (TRAID Project) Center
- Center for Assistive Technology (CAT)
- Rehabilitation Engineering and Assistive Technology Society of North America (RESNA)
- Office of Advocate for Persons with Disabilities (OAPwD)

The federal act, Individuals with Disabilities Education Act (IDEA) (Public Law 101-476), "explains the Assistive Technology Devices and Services that can be used in an educational setting. For example, IDEA is administered in each state usually by the Department of Education, but sometimes by the state's Department of Health, for children from birth to age 3 and by the Department of Education for children ages 3 through and including age 21.

Examples of **Assistive Technology Devices and Services** include:

1. **Computers with Software/Hardware Adaptations:** Braille printers, voice output, voice-activated computers, large screens, touch screens, computer access by body movements other than traditional keyboard and mouse.
2. **Assistive Listening Devices:** Hearing aids, radio transmission (FM) devices, closed caption TV, TTY (Teletypewriter) and TDD (Telecommunication Device for the Deaf) and volume-amplified telephones to light signalers, loud tone ringers, and large-number and hands-free telephones. For recorded information about the Verizon program or to request an application, call 1 (800) 882-6828 (V, Voice) or 1 (800) 299-2640 (TTY). To qualify for the free Verizon assistive equipment, your child must be under 18 years old and have a certified disability that hinders him (or her) from using the phone, and receive SSI disability benefits.
3. **Classroom Modifications:** Adaptive seating/positioning technology devices.

Assistive technology devices and services can be approved on the IEP if they are needed to allow the child to achieve reasonable educational progress in the least restrictive setting. This would allow the student to remain in the regular classroom setting. If the assistive technology devices and services have been approved by the CSE on the IEP, according to the United States Department of Education, the school district is specifically required to purchase the assistive technology devices and services and pay for any training, maintenance and repair of these devices. Any assistive technology device purchased by the school district usually remains the property of the school district, even if the student moves away.

Medicaid or Private Insurance *may be used* for the purchase of assistive technology devices and services. Use of these payment sources is voluntary and must be done with the parents' knowledge and permission. Parents must ask if using private insurance limits future coverage for other family use. Use of private insurance or Medicaid does not legally relieve the school district from implementing and delivering all IEP services.

There is no restriction in federal law preventing the family from taking assistive technology devices home and receiving necessary training if it is needed for the benefit of the child. This should be discussed in the CSE meeting and documented on the IEP.

Section 504 of the Federal Rehabilitation Act. Some students with a recognizable disability *may not* qualify or require all the special education services, such as physical, occupational and speech therapies. However, these students may indeed need specified therapies or assistive technology devices and services to fully participate in school activities. In accordance with **Section 504 of the Federal Rehabilitation Act,** school districts are required by federal law to ensure that students with disabilities are not discriminated against in gaining access to the full range of programs and activities offered by the school. As with special education services, it is the school district's legal responsibility to pay for assistive technology devices and services including training, repairs and maintenance provided under Section 504 of the Federal Rehabilitation Act. Therefore, some students are *not legally required* to be labeled or classified by the CSE on an IEP as a student with a disability in order to receive assistive technology devices or services.

Assistive technology is rapidly changing. For more information on adaptive technology devices and services, contact:

Alliance for Technology Access
2175 E. Francisco Blvd., Suite L
San Rafael, CA 94901
Phone: (415) 455-4575
E-mail: ATAinfo@ATAaccess.org
Web site: www.ATAaccess.org

The many government agencies supporting special education, assistive technology services and devices as well as research and special programs can be confusing. Within the **United States Department of Education** is the **Office of Special Education and Rehabilitation Services (OSERS)** Web site: www.ed.gov/offices/OSERS

The **Office of Special Education and Rehabilitative Services (OSERS)** supports programs that assist in educating children with special needs, provides for the rehabilitation of youth and adults with disabilities, and supports research to improve the lives of individuals with disabilities.

To carry out its duties, **OSERS** consists of three program-related components: the **Office of Special Education Programs (OSEP)**, the **Rehabilitation Services Administration (RSA)**, and the **National Institute on Disability and Rehabilitation Research (NIDRR)**.

The **Office of Special Education Programs (OSEP)** has primary responsibility for administering programs and projects relating to the free appropriate public education of all children, youth and adults with disabilities, from birth through age 21. The bulk of special education funds is administered by **OSEP's** Monitoring and State Improvement Programs division, which provides grants to states and territories to assist them in providing a free, appropriate public education to all children with disabilities. The early intervention and preschool grant programs provide grants to each state for children with disabilities, ages birth through five.

The **Office of Special Education Programs (OSEP)** Web site is: www.ed.gov/offices/OSERS/OSEP/index.html.

The **Rehabilitation Services Administration (RSA)** oversees programs that help individuals with physical or mental disabilities to obtain employment through the provision of such supports as counseling, medical and psychological services, job training, and other individualized services. The **RSA's** major formula grant program provides funds to state vocational rehabilitation agencies to provide employment-related services for individuals with disabilities, giving priority to individuals who are severely disabled.

The **Rehabilitation Services Administration (RSA)** Web site is: www.ed.gov/offices/OSERS/RSA/index.html.

The third component of **OSERS** is the **National Institute on Disability and Rehabilitation Research (NIDRR)**, which provides leadership and support for a comprehensive program of research related to the rehabilitation of individuals with disabilities. All of the programmatic efforts are aimed at improving the lives of individuals with disabilities from birth through adulthood.

The **National Institute on Disability and Rehabilitation Research (NIDRR)** Web site is: www.ed.gov/offices/OSERS/NIDRR/.

Regarding the individual state assistive technology programs, they are funded with grants, in accordance with Assistive Technology Act of 1998 (Public Law 105-394). For more general information on **Assistive Technology Devices and Services** or for specific state information on the nearest **Regional Technology Related Assistance for Individuals with Disabilities (TRAID Project) Center,** frequently called a **Center for Assistive Technology (CAT),** contact the **Rehabilitation Engineering and Assistive Technology Society of North America (RESNA):**

RESNA Technical Assistance Project
1700 N. Moore Street
Suite 1540
Arlington, VA 22209-1903
Phone: (703) 524-6686 (voice), (703) 524-6639 (TTY)
Fax: (703) 524-6630
E-mail: info@resna.org
Web site: www.resna.org

For example, in the Western New York area, the **Regional Technology Related Assistance for Individuals with Disabilities (TRAID Project) Center,** called the **Center for Assistive Technology (CAT),** is:

The Center for Assistive Technology (CAT)
University at Buffalo
515 Kimball Tower
3435 Main Street
Toll Free: (800) 628-2281 (voice/TTY), Phone: (716) 829-3141 (voice/TTY)
E-mail: jweir@buffalo.edu
Web site: www.wings.buffalo.edu/ot/cat

Like other CAT programs across the United States, the Center for Assistive Technology at the University at Buffalo provides an assessment for assistive technology and training services for school-age children in Western New York on a fee-for-service basis. The Committee for Special Education (CSE) chairperson of the student's school makes referral to the CAT. The CAT assessment team works closely with the student, family and school team members to define daily activities and educational tasks for which assistive technology would likely increase functional ability. Recommendations are made in writing from the CAT assessment team for specific assistive technology devices (hardware and software). If the equipment is purchased, the CAT assessment team provides equipment setup and training for the student, family and school team members on a fee-for-service basis.

By contacting your state's local Center for Assistive Technology (CAT), using the RESNA Technical Assistance Project information above, you can request a referral package for an "Assistive Technology Assessment from the CAT Assessment Team for School-aged Children" in the your area. Your local Center for Assistive Technology (CAT) and the TRAID Project is also funded under Public Law 100-407 by grants from the National Institute on Disability and Rehabilitation Research (NIDRR), U.S. Department of Education.

Often, each state's federally funded TRAID project or CAT program will assist a parent in developing strategies to acquire needed assistive technology devices and services as well as consumer tips on buying these services and devices and various funding sources. These resource materials are offered in Spanish, Braille, and large print, on diskette and on audiocassette.

To search your state's Web site to locate information on the federally funded TRAID project close to your home, or special education issues on your child's specific disability, go to your state's individual Web site: www.state.(then type the U.S. mail two-letter abreviation for your state, like IL for Illinois).us. For example, the state of Illinois' Web site would be www.state.IL.us. You can then search your state's Web site for specific topics on adaptive technology devices and services related to your child's specific disability.

For example, in New York State, the TRAID project is administered by the **New York State Office of Advocate for Persons with Disabilities (OAPwD)**:

New York Office of Advocate for Persons with Disabilities (OAPwD)
One Empire State Plaza, Suite 1001
Albany, NY 12223-1150
Phone: (800) 522-4369 (Voice/TTY, Spanish); (518) 474-2825 (Voice);
(518) 473-4231 (TTY)
Fax: (518) 473-6005; (800)-943-2323 (BBS)
E-mail: information@oapwd.state.ny.us
Web site: www.advoc4disabled.state.ny.us.

Due Process Rights for Parents of Children with Disabilities

(New York State Edition)

As legally required by the United States Department of Education, parents of children with disabilities must be provided a copy of the most currently revised, Mandatory State Procedural Safeguards Notice. The *New York State Due Process Rights for Parents of Children with Disabilities, Procedural Safeguard Notice (January 2002 re*vision, reproduced with permission) is enclosed as a well-written, comprehensive example with easily defined legal terms. We recommended you contact your local school board's Department of Education for the most current copy of your state's equivalent of the Mandatory State Procedural Safeguards Notice.

New York State Education Department
PROCEDURAL SAFEGUARDS NOTICE

- Procedural Safeguard Notice Defined
- Consent
- Notices: Prior Notices and Meeting Notices
- Your Child's Educational Records
- Evaluations: Independent Education Evaluation (IEE)
- Complaints
- Special Education Mediation
- Impartial Due Process Hearing
- Court Appeal
- Pendency: The Student's Placement During Due Process Hearing
- Interim Alternative Educational Setting (IAES)
- Attorneys Fees
- Reimbursement: Private Schooling
- Disciplinary Procedures

New York State Education Department
PROCEDURAL SAFEGUARDS NOTICE

Rights for Parents of Children with Disabilities, Ages 3-21

Parents are vital members of a team called the Committee on Special Education (CSE) or Committee on Preschool Special Education (CPSE) that is responsible for developing an appropriate educational program for your child. You must be given opportunities to participate in the discussion and decision making process about your child's needs for special education. The following information concerns procedural safeguards—your legal rights under federal and State laws to be involved and make sure that your child receives a free appropriate public education.

Procedural safeguards notice is provided:
- upon initial referral for evaluation of your child.
- with each notice of a CSE or CPSE meeting.
- upon reevaluation of your child.
- when the district receives a letter from you requesting an impartial hearing.
- when a decision is made to suspend or remove your child for discipline reasons that would result in a disciplinary change in placement.

CONSENT
There are many times when the school district must notify (tell) you in writing of its proposed (planned) action and ask for your written consent (permission) to carry out this action.

<u>Consent</u> means that:
1. you have been informed, in the language you speak or other kind of communication that you understand, of all the information about the activity for which your permission is asked.
2. you understand and agree in writing to the activity for which your permission is needed.

3. your permission is given freely and may be withdrawn at any time. However, if you withdraw your consent, it is not retroactive (it will not apply to actions already taken by the district).

Your consent will be requested when:

1. your child will be evaluated for the first time by the Committee to decide if he or she has a disability and needs special education.
2. your child is recommended to receive special education services and programs for the first time.
3. your child is recommended to receive twelve-month special education services and/or programs during July and August for the first time.
4. your child will be reevaluated.
5. the school district proposes to use your private insurance. In this case, you must be notified that, if you refuse to allow the school district to access (use) your private insurance, the district is still responsible to provide all required services at no cost to you.
6. another agency other than a school requests to review records about your child. The request for consent will include information about the records that will be released and to whom they will be given.

NOTICES: Prior Notice and Meeting Notice

As a parent of a child with a disability or suspected disability, you will receive notices to tell you about proposed special education services, meetings and your rights. Notice is a written statement provided to you in the language you speak or other kind of communication that you understand unless it is clearly not possible to do so. If the language you speak at home (your native language) or other kind of communication you understand is not a written language, the district must take steps to make sure that the notice is translated orally or by other means (such as sign language) so that you understand the notice. You have the right to ask for an interpreter, translator or reader for the meetings.

In addition to this procedural safeguards notice, you will also receive:

• prior notices and
• notices of meetings.

Prior Notice

Prior notice is written notice that is given to you a reasonable time before the school district proposes to or refuses to start or change the identification, evaluation or educational placement or the provision of a free appropriate education to your child.

Prior Notice must include:

1. a description of the action offered or refused by the CSE or CPSE.
2. an explanation of why the school district will or will not take action.
3. a description of any other options (choices) the school district considered and the reasons why those choices were refused.
4. a description of each evaluation, procedure, test, record or report the school district used as a reason to offer or refuse an action.
5. a description of any other factors that are relevant to the district's decision.
6. a statement that you have protection under the law. This legal protection is called procedural safeguards and they are listed in the procedural safeguards notice. If the procedural safeguards notice is not included with the prior notice, the prior notice will describe the ways you can obtain (get) a copy of a description of the procedural safeguards.
7. sources for you to contact to get assistance in understanding the special education process and your rights.

If the prior notice relates to an action by the school district that requires your consent, the district will give you notice at the same time they request your consent. You should also receive prior notice before your child graduates from high school with a local or Regents diploma or before he/she receives an Individualized Education Program (IEP) diploma.

Notice of Meetings

Whenever the Committee proposes to conduct a meeting to develop or review your child's IEP or to discuss the provision of a free appropriate public education to your child, you must receive a meeting notice.

You must receive a written meeting notice at least five days before the meeting unless you and the school district agree to meet within five days or in certain meetings relating to discipline procedures. If the proposed meeting time or place is not good for you, you may call the school district to ask for a change that is good for both of you.

If you are unable to attend the meeting, the district can use other ways to encourage your participation. They may call you before a meeting occurs to talk about evaluation results and ask you for information, or they may ask you to participate in the meeting by telephone.

A Meeting Notice must include:

1. the purpose of the meeting and the date, time, location and names and titles of the persons expected to attend the meeting.
2. a statement that you have the right to participate as a member of the Committee.
3. a statement telling you that you may bring anyone to the meeting who has knowledge or special expertise about your child.
4. a statement of your right to ask the school physician to be at the meeting of the CSE. (This does not apply to parents of preschool children.) You must do this in writing at least 72 hours before the meeting.
5. a statement that you may request in writing that the additional parent member of the Committee not participate in the meeting of the Committee.
6. if the meeting is a Subcommittee meeting, a statement that you may make a written request to the full Committee if you disagree with the recommendation of a Subcommittee.
7. for students for whom a meeting will be held to consider transition services, a statement that indicates the purpose of the meeting and that the student will be invited and lists any other agencies that will be invited to send a representative.
8. for preschool students, a statement that you have the opportunity to address the Preschool Committee in writing or in person.

YOUR CHILD'S EDUCATIONAL RECORDS

You have the right to ask for and read records about your child unless the district has been legally notified in writing that your rights as a parent have been terminated or otherwise limited by a court order.

You have the right to ask for and receive explanations and interpretations of the records from your school district. You also have the right to ask that the school district provide you with a copy of your child's educational records if *it is* the only way that you can inspect and review the records. The school district may charge a reasonable cost for copies of the records unless the fee prevents you from inspecting or reviewing your child's records. You may also have your representative inspect and review the records. Upon your request, the school district must allow you to review and inspect your child's records:

- within a reasonable time.
- in no case more than 45 calendar days after you ask.
- before any meeting about your child's IEP.
- before any due process hearing about your child's special education needs.

Personal information about your child may not be released without your consent unless it is:

1. given to school officials or teachers with a legitimate educational interest, State and local educational authorities, or certain individuals designated under federal law.
2. used to meet a requirement under federal law.

EVALUATIONS

Individual evaluation

An individual evaluation means any procedures, tests or assessments, including observations, given individually to your child to find out whether he or she has a disability and/or to identify his/her special education needs. The term does not include basic tests given to groups of children in a school, grade or class.

The results of the evaluation must be shared with you. When the CSE or CPSE has conducted an evaluation to determine your child's eligibility for special education, you must be provided a copy of the evaluation report and documentation of determination of eligibility. In addition, if you are the parent of a preschool child, the CPSE must also give you a copy of the summary report of the findings of the evaluation.

Independent Educational Evaluation

An independent educational evaluation (IEE) of your child means a procedure, test or assessment done by a qualified examiner who does not work for the school district or other public agency responsible for the child's education. You may get an IEE at district expense if you disagree with the evaluation arranged for by the school district. If you ask the school district to pay for the IEE, the school district may ask, but not require, you to explain the reason why you object to the district's evaluation. The school district may not unreasonably delay either providing the IEE or initiating an impartial hearing to defend the district's evaluation.

Independent evaluators (outside testers) must meet the same qualifications as school district evaluators and follow the accepted evaluation procedures.

You have the right to:

1. obtain an independent educational evaluation (IEE).
2. have the results of the IEE considered by the CSE or CPSE as part of its review and in the development of your child's IEP.
3. have the full cost of the IEE be at district expense. The school district may request an impartial hearing to show that its evaluation is appropriate or that your evaluation did not follow district criteria. If the impartial hearing officer (IHO) finds that the district evaluation is appropriate, the district does not have to pay for it.
4. receive information about where an IEE may be obtained, the criteria the school district uses when it does an evaluation, and any district criteria regarding the reimbursement of IEEs if you request the district pay for the IEE.
5. have an IEE at district expense if the IHO asks for this evaluation as part of an impartial hearing.
6. have the results of the IEE used as evidence at an impartial hearing.

OPPORTUNITY TO PRESENT COMPLAINTS

You have the right to submit a written complaint to the New York State Education Department if you believe that your school district has violated procedures under State or federal special education laws and regulations. Your complaint must include a statement that the school district has violated special education law or regulations and include the facts on which you base your statement. You must send the original signed written complaint to:

Coordinator, Statewide Special Education
Quality Assurance
Office of Vocational and Educational Services
for Individuals with Disabilities
One Commerce Plaza, Room 1619
Albany, NY 12234

The alleged violation must have occurred not more than one year prior to the date of the complaint:

- unless the violation is continuing; or
- the complaint is requesting compensation services. This only applies to alleged violations that occurred not more than three years prior to the date of the complaint.

A determination must be made within 60 calendar days of receipt of the complaint unless exceptional circumstances exist.

SPECIAL EDUCATION MEDIATION

Special education mediation is a voluntary process for you and the school district which all school districts must offer parents as a way to work out disagreements with the recommendations of the CPSE/CSE. You and a person chosen by the Board of Education (BOE) meet with a qualified and impartial mediator from the Community Dispute Resolution Center (CDRC) who helps in reaching agreement about the recommendation for your child. Mediation is at no cost to you. If you decide to use mediation, you must ask for it by writing to the BOE. If you decide not to use mediation, someone may call you from the CDRC to talk about the benefits of mediation.

You have the right to:
1. mediation by a qualified and impartial mediator from a CDRC.
2. mediation held in a timely manner and at a place that is good for you and the district.
3. have any agreements made during mediation written down. Written agreements may be presented as part of the record at an impartial hearing.

4. have discussions that occur during the mediation process be confidential and not used as evidence in any impartial hearing or civil proceedings. Parties to the mediation process may be required to sign a confidentiality pledge prior to the mediation.
5. request an impartial hearing at any time.

IMPARTIAL DUE PROCESS HEARING

An impartial hearing is a formal proceeding in which disagreements between you and the school district are decided by an impartial hearing officer (IHO) appointed by the BOE.

1. Your request for an impartial hearing must be made in writing to the BOE.
2. You must also provide written notice that describes the facts relating to your concerns and a proposed solution and states your child's name, address and the name of the school your child attends. A form can be obtained from your local school district to request an impartial hearing or mediation. If you do not give the information stated above, it may result in a reduction of an award of attorneys' fees by a court.
3. An impartial hearing may be initiated by you or the BOE if the CPSE/CSE proposes or refuses to start, continue or change the identification, evaluation or educational placement of your child or the provision of a free appropriate public education (FAPE) to your child.
4. For school-age children, the school district must begin an impartial hearing when you refuse to give consent for:
   • an initial evaluation (During the 30-day period, the district must provide you an opportunity for an informal conference to discuss the request for an initial evaluation and the request may be subsequently withdrawn.);
   • the initial provision of special education to your child; or
   • the initial provision of a twelve-month special education service and/or program to your child.
5. For school-age children, the school district may begin an impartial hearing when you refuse to give consent for a reevaluation of your child.
6. For three- and four-year-old children, the school district may not begin a hearing if you refuse to give consent to initial evaluation,

initial provision of special education or the initial provision of a twelve-month special education service and/or program to your child.

7. The impartial hearing is at no cost to you. You may have to pay your own attorneys' fees. When you request an impartial hearing, the school district must inform you of any free or low-cost legal and other relevant services in the area.

At an impartial due process hearing, you have the right to:

1. have and be advised by an attorney and/or by individuals with special knowledge or training about the education of students with disabilities.
2. present evidence and testimony and question, cross-examine and require the attendance of witnesses.
3. receive information, including evaluations and recommendations, at least five business days before the hearing (or three business days in the case of an expedited due process hearing) and to stop such information from being presented that was not exchanged between both parties on time.
4. receive, at your option, a written or electronic word-for-word record of the hearing and word-for-word findings of fact and the decision of the IHO.
5. have the hearing open to the public.
6. have your child present during the hearing.
7. have an interpreter for the deaf or an interpreter fluent in your native language (the language normally used by you), if necessary, at no cost to you.
8. have an impartial hearing conducted at a time and place that is reasonably convenient for you and your child.
9. receive an expedited due process hearing for certain disciplinary decisions.

Timelines for impartial hearings

1. The decision of an IHO in an impartial hearing must be issued no later than 45 calendar days after the receipt of a request for a hearing for a school-age child or 30 calendar days for a preschool child. However, the IHO may extend the time for a specific period at the request of you or the school district.

2. The decision of an IHO in an expedited due process hearing for discipline purposes must be completed within 15 business days after the receipt of the request for the hearing, provided that the IHO may grant specific extensions at your or the school district's request. The IHO must mail a written decision to the parties within five business days after the last hearing date, but in no event later than 45 calendar days after receipt of the request, without exceptions or extensions.

STATE-LEVEL APPEAL OF IHO DECISIONS

The decision made by the IHO is final unless you or the school district ask for a review of the decision of the IHO (called an appeal) by the State Review Officer (SRO). If you want to appeal the IHO's decision to the State Review Officer, a notice of intention to seek review of the decision must be served upon the school district within 30 days of receipt of the IHO'S decision. Ten calendar days after serving the notice of intention, a petition for review must be served upon the school district. A board of education must serve its petition within 40 calendar days after receipt of the IHO decision. The original petition for review must be mailed or delivered to the State Education Department. Additional rules for filing an appeal to the SRO can be found at http://seddmznt.nysed.gov/sro/part279.htm.

The State Review Officer (SRO) will:

1. make sure that steps taken at the hearing agree with due process requirements.
2. obtain additional evidence, if necessary. If a hearing is held for the purpose of obtaining additional evidence, all the parent rights listed under impartial hearings continue. Such a hearing must be held at a time and place that is reasonably convenient to you and your child and the school district.
3. hear oral argument if the SRO decides it is necessary. Such argument must be held at a time and place that is reasonably convenient to you and your child and the school district.
4. make an independent decision after a complete review of the hearing record.
5. make a final decision within 30 calendar days after receiving the request (petition) for a review. The SRO may extend the time

beyond the 30 days at the request of you or the school district. The extension must be for a specific time.

6. mail copies of the written or, at your option, electronic findings of fact and the decision to you or your attorney and the BOE within the 30-day period.

COURT APPEAL OF SRO DECISION

The decision of the SRO is final unless either you or the school district seeks review of the SRO's decision in either State Supreme Court or Federal District Court within four months from the date of the SRO's decision.

PENDENCY: THE STUDENT'S PLACEMENT DURING DUE PROCESS HEARINGS

During any impartial hearing or appeal, your child will remain in his or her current educational placement. This is sometimes referred to as "pendency," "stay-put," or "status-quo."

Preschool child

Your preschool child will stay in his or her current placement during any hearing or appeal, unless you and the school district agree in writing to other arrangements.

A child who has received early intervention services and is now of preschool age may, during hearings and appeals, receive special education in the same program as the early intervention program if that program is also an approved preschool program.

If your preschool child is currently not receiving special education services and programs, he or she may, during any hearings or appeals, receive special education services and programs if you and the school district agree.

School-age child

During any hearing or appeal, your school-age child will stay in the school placement he or she is in now, unless you and the school district agree in writing to other arrangements.

If the disagreement involves initial admission to public school, you have the right to have your school-age child placed in a public school program with your consent until all proceedings are over.

If the due process proceeding concerns consent for an initial evaluation, your child will not be evaluated while the proceeding is pending.

A child who received preschool special education services and is now school age may, during hearings and appeals, remain in the same program as the preschool program if that program also has an approved school-age special education program.

Court Appeal of SRO Decision

If you or the school is appealing a decision of a State Review Officer to a court, pendency is as follows:

- If a State Review Officer issues a placement decision that agrees with the parents, pendency during any subsequent appeal to a court is the placement decided by the State Review Officer.
- If the State Review Officer issues a placement decision that agrees with the school district, pendency during any subsequent appeal to a court is your child's current educational placement.

Interim Alternative Educational Setting (IAES) for Discipline Purposes

If your child is receiving services in an IAES for discipline purposes, he or she must remain in that IAES until an impartial hearing officer makes a determination about placement or until the end of the 45 calendar days, whichever occurs first, unless you and the school district otherwise agree.

- However, if the Committee proposes to change the placement at the end of the IAES and you challenge the proposed change in placement, pendency for your child will be the current educational placement (placement prior to removal to the IAES).
- An impartial hearing officer may place your child in an IAES again because the school district believes that it is dangerous for the student to stay in his or her current educational placement.

ATTORNEY'S FEES

A court may award reasonable attorneys' fees to the parents or guardian of a child with a disability if they are the party who wins the hearing. Attorneys' fees may be lowered if you unreasonably delay an agreement or a decision in the case; if the fees, time spent or services of your attorney exceed reasonable rates; or if you failed to provide the information required when you request a hearing. However, attorneys' fees will not be reduced if a court finds that the State or school district unreasonably delayed the final resolution of the action or proceeding or there was a violation of your child's due process rights. Attorneys' fees may not be awarded:

- relating to any meeting of the CSE or CPSE unless the meeting is held as a result of an administrative proceeding or court action.
- for mediation that is conducted prior to the filing of a request for an impartial hearing.
- if a written offer of settlement is made by the school district within ten calendar days prior to the proceeding, you do not accept the offer within ten calendar days and the court or hearing officer finds that the decision is not more favorable to the parents than the offer of settlement.

REIMBURSEMENT FOR PLACEMENT MADE BY PARENTS IN A PRIVATE SCHOOL IF THE DISTRICT FAILS TO MAKE A FREE AND APPROPRIATE PROGRAM AVAILABLE TO THE CHILD

A school district is not required to pay for the cost of education of your child at a private school or facility if the school district has made a free and appropriate public education (FAPE) available to your child. However, if you place your child in a private school because you and the school district disagree that an appropriate program has been made available for your child, you have the right to request an impartial hearing to seek reimbursement for the private school placement.

1. If you are the parent of a child who previously received a special education program and/or services through the school district and you place your child in a private school without the consent or referral of the school district, you may be entitled to reimbursement for the cost of the private placement if you can prove at an impartial hearing or State-level or court appeal that:
    - the school district did not provide your child with a free appropriate public education in a timely manner prior to that enrollment in private school: and

- the private placement is appropriate to meet your child's educational needs. A hearing officer or court may find that a parental placement is appropriate even if it does not meet the State standards that apply to education programs provided by the school district or the State.

2. Your reimbursement may be denied or reduced if you do not:
   - inform the school district at the most recent CSE or CPSE meeting you attend that you are rejecting the placement proposed by the school district and state your concerns and that you will be placing your child at a private school at public expense, or
   - provide the school district with written notice at least ten business days (including any holidays that occur on a business day) prior to removing your child from the public school. However, if you are unable to read and cannot write in English; or if providing notice would likely result in physical or serious emotional harm to your child; or if the school prevented you from providing the notice; or if you did not receive the procedural safeguards notice that tells you about this requirement, then the cost of reimbursement may not be reduced or denied because you did not give this notice.

3. If the school district gave you written notice prior to your removing your child from public school that it wants to evaluate your child, you must make your child available for the evaluation. If you refuse to make your child available, any request for tuition reimbursement may be reduced or denied.

4. If you do not inform the school district or make your child available for the evaluation, or if there are other unreasonable actions on your part, an impartial hearing officer or court may reduce or deny the reimbursement of costs of the private school for your child.

DISCIPLINARY PROCEDURES

The procedures for the discipline of students with disabilities must be in accordance with section 3214 of the Education Law and Part 201 of the Regulations of the Commissioner of Education. While the school has the authority to suspend or remove your child for violating the school's code of conduct, you and your child have certain rights throughout the process.

You have the right:

1. to be notified immediately by telephone, if possible, and to receive written notice within 24 hours of a proposed suspension of five school days or less. The notice should describe the incident, proposed suspension and your child's rights. You also have the right to request an informal conference with the school principal prior to the suspension unless your child's presence in school poses a danger.

2. to receive written notice of your opportunity for a superintendent's hearing, if the suspension is for more than five consecutive school days, which describes your child's rights to counsel and to question and present witnesses.

3. for your child to receive alternative instruction during the first ten days of any suspension or removal to the same extent as nondisabled students, if your child is of compulsory school age.

4. for your child to receive education services necessary to enable your child to progress in the general education curriculum and appropriately advance toward achieving his or her IEP goals if your child is suspended or removed for more than ten school days in a school year.

5. for your child also to have services to address the behavior that resulted in the disciplinary action if your child is removed to an interim alternative educational setting.

6. to have the CSE develop or review and implement a behavioral intervention plan for your child that is based on the results of a functional behavioral assessment, if your child is suspended or removed for more than ten school days in a school year.

7. to a CSE meeting to determine whether your child's behavior which led to the disciplinary action is related to his or her disability (manifestation determination) when the suspension or removal results in your child being suspended or removed for more than ten school days in a school year (disciplinary change in placement).

8. for your child not to be suspended or removed for behaviors that are determined to be related to your child's disability, except for suspensions or removals ten school days or less in a school year and for removals to interim alternative educational settings.

9. to challenge, in an expedited due process hearing before an impartial hearing officer, the decision of the CSE regarding the relationship between your child's behavior that resulted in a disciplinary action and his or her disability (manifestation determination).

10. to challenge, in an expedited due process hearing before an impartial hearing officer, any placement decision related to discipline.

Interim Alternative Educational Settings

1. Controlled Substances/Illegal Drugs/Weapons: School authorities may remove your child to an interim alternative educational setting for up to 45 calendar days if your child carries or possesses a weapon to or at school, on school premises, or to a school function, or knowingly possesses or uses illegal drugs or sells or solicits the sale of a controlled substance while at school or a school function.

2. *Dangerousness:* An impartial hearing officer may order the removal of your child to an interim alternative educational setting in a dangerous situation (i.e., maintaining the student in the current educational placement is substantially likely to result in injury to your child or to others).

3. An *interim alternative education setting* is a temporary educational placement for a period of up to 45 calendar days, other than your child's current placement, that:
   • enables your child to continue to progress in the general education curriculum;
   • provides services and modifications described in the IEP to meet the IEP goals; and
   • includes services and modifications to address the behavior that resulted in the disciplinary action and are designed to prevent the behavior from reoccurring.

4. As a parent, you have the right to challenge, in an expedited due process hearing, the decision to place your child in an interim alternative educational setting. During this process, unless you and the school district otherwise agree to another placement, your child will remain in the interim alternative educational setting until the period of time of the removal expires, but not more

than 45 days. However, an impartial hearing officer can extend the placement in the interim alternative educational setting.

Students with disabilities, students presumed to have a disability for discipline purposes, and students referred for special education while subject to disciplinary action.

1. *Students with disabilities*: A student who has been identified by a CSE or a CPSE as a student with a disability must be afforded all the due process rights in this notice.

2. *Students presumed to have a disability*: If you believe that the school district had knowledge that your child was a child with a disability prior to the behavior that resulted in the disciplinary action, you have the right to assert that your child is a *student presumed to have a disability*. If it is determined that the district did, in fact, have such knowledge, then your child has all the rights and protections in this notice.

3. *Students not yet identified as a student with a disability*: If you request an initial evaluation of your child during the time period in which your child is suspended or removed for disciplinary reasons, the evaluation must be conducted in an expedited manner (completed no later than 15 school days after you request the evaluation). The CSE meeting to determine eligibility must be held no later than five school days after the completion of the expedited evaluation. Until the evaluation is completed, your child remains in the educational placement determined by school authorities, which can include suspension.

Adaptive Equipment Companies in the U.S. and Canada

AdaptABILITY
P.O. Box 513
Colchester, CT 06415-0513
Phone: (800) 243-9232
E-mail: service@ snswwide.com
Web site: www.snswwide.com
*Equipment for independent living

Ball Dynamics International, Inc.
14215 Mead Street
Longmont, CO 80504Phone: (800) 752-2255
Fax: (877) 223-2962
Web site: www.balldynamics.com
*Therapeutic balls and seating equipment

Best Priced Products, Inc.
P.O. Box 1174
White Plains, NY 10602
Phone: (800) 824-2939, 914-591-6900
Fax: (800) 356-8587, 914-591-3208
E-mail: customerservice@Best-Priced-Products.com
Web site: www.Best-Priced-Products.com
*exercise and physical/occupation therapy equipment

Otto Bock Orthopedic Industry, USA
3000 Xenium Lane North
Minneapolis, MN 55441
Phone: (800) 328-4058, (612) 553-9464
Fax: (800) 962-2549
E-mail: info@ottoblockus.com
Web site: www.ottobockus.com
*Orthotics and specialized wheelchairs

Otto Bock Orthopedic Industry of Canada Ltd.
2897 Brighton RoadOakville, Ontario L6W 5S3
Phone: (905) 829-2080
Fax: (905) 829-1811
E-mail: ottobock@idirect.com
Web site: www.ottobockus.com
*Orthotics and specialized wheelchairs

Consumer Care, Inc.
Rehab Specialties Division
1446 Pilgrim RoadPlymouth, WI 53073
Phone: (920) 893-4614
Fax: (800) 977-2256
E-mail: ccpi@consumercareinc.com
Web site: www.consumercareinc.com
*Unique rehabilitation equipment and supplies for exceptional persons

DANMAR Products, Inc.
221 Jackson Industrial Drive
Ann Arbor, MI 48103
Phone: (800) 783-1998
Fax: (734) 761-8977
E-mail: salesdepartment@danmarproducts.com
Web site: www.danmarproducts.com
*Designing special products and adaptive equipment

Equipment Shop
P.O. Box 33
Bedford, MA 01730
Phone: (800) 525-7681, (781) 275-7681
Fax: (781) 275-4094
Web site: www.equipmentshop.com
*Special pediatric equipment for therapy and exercise.

Gunnell, Inc.
221 North Water Street
P.O. Box 1694
Vassar, MI 48768-9986
Phone: (800) 551-0055
Fax: (517) 871-4563
E-mail: info@gunnell-inc.com
Web site: www.gunnell-inc.com
*Individualized wheelchairs and versatile seating systems

Kaye Products Inc.
535 Dimmocks Mill Road
Hillsborough, NC 27278
Phone: (800) 685-5293, (919) 732-6444
Fax: (919) 732-1444
Web site: www.kayeproducts.com
*Adaptive equipment and products for Activities of Daily Living (ADL)

G.E. Miller, Inc.
45 Saw Mill River Road
Yonkers, NY 10701
Phone: (800) 431-2924
Fax: (914) 969-3511
Web site: www.gemiller.com
*Rehabilitation equipment

Mulholland Positioning Systems
P.O. Box 391
215 North 12th Street
Santa Paula, CA 93061
Phone: (800) 543-4769, (805) 525-7165
Fax: (805) 933-1082
E-mail: webmaster@mulhollandinc.com
Web site: www.mulhollandinc.com
*Positioning rehabilitation equipment

Ortho-Kinetics and Lark of America
W220 N507 Springdale Road
Waukesha, WI 53187
Phone: (800) 558-7786, (800) 446-4522, (800) 522-0992 (in Wisconsin)
Web site: www.orthokinetics.com
*Pediatric rehabilitation/mobility equipment and Lark Scooters

Sammons Preston
Ability One Corporation
4 Sammons Court
Bolingbrook, IL 60440
Phone: (800) 323-5547 and (800) 665-9200 in Canada
Fax: (800) 547-4333
Web site: www.sammonspreston.com
*Rehabilitation equipment

Southpaw Enterprises
P.O. Box 1047
Dayton, OH 45401-1047
Phone: (800) 228-1698
E-mail: therapy@southpawenterprises.com
Web site: www.southpawenterprises.com
*Equipment for sensory integration and neuro-developmental products

Sunrise Medical
Jay Medical/Longmont
7477A E. Dry Creek Parkway
Longmont, CO 80503
Phone: (800) 648-8282

Sunrise Medical Canada
237 Romina Drive, Unit 3
Concord, Ontario L4K 4V3 Canada
Phone: (905) 660-6704
Fax: (905) 660-2460
Web site: www.sunrisemedicalonline.com and www.sunrisemedical.com
*Seating systems, adjustable cushions, seats, adaptive strollers and wheel-chairs

TherAdapt Products, Inc.
17 West 163 Oak Lane
Bensenville, IL 60106
Phone: (800) 261-4919, (603) 834-2461
Fax: (603) 834-2478
E-mail: mail@theradapt.com
Web site: www.theradapt.com
*Innovative early intervention and school-aged pediatric therapeutic equip-ment

National Programs and Information Centers in the U.S. and Canada

National Programs and Information Centers, listed alphabetically, followed by Expanded Information for the following organizations, programs and information centers:

- Autism Organizations
- Cerebral Palsy Organizations
- Dental Services
- Nonverbal Learning Disorder (NLD or NVLD)
- Nutritional Needs
- Parent Advocacy Center for Educational Rights (PACER) Center Speech and Communication
- Supplemental Security Income (SSI)
- United States Department of Education

American Association on Mental Retardation
444 North Capitol Street, NW Suite 846
Washington, D.C. 20001-1512
Phone: (800) 424-3688, (202) 387-1968
Fax: (202) 387-2193
Web site: www.aamr.org

American Diabetes Association
National Office1701 North Beauregard StreetAlexandria, VA 22311
Phone: (800) DIABETES (342-2383)
E-mail: customerservice@diabetes.org
Web site: www.diabetes.org

American Foundation for the Blind, Inc.
11 Penn Plaza
New York, NY 10001
Phone: (800) AFB-LINE (232-5463); (202) 502-7600
E-mail: afbinfor@afb.org
Web site: www.afb.org

American Orthotic and Prosthetic Association
1650 King Street, Suite 500
Alexandria, VA 22314
Phone: (703) 836-7116
Fax: (703) 836-0838
E-mail: info@aopanet.org
Web site: www.aopanet.org

The Arc of the United States
(formerly National Association for Retarded Citizens)
National Headquarters Office
1010 Wayne Ave.,
Suite 650
Silver Spring, MD 20910
Phone: (301) 565-3842
Fax: (301) 565-5342
E-mail: Info@thearc.org
Web site: www.thearc.org

Arthritis Foundation
1330 West Peachtree Street
Atlanta, GA 30309
Phone: (800) 783-7800; (404) 872-7100
E-mail: help@arthritis.org
Web site: www.arthritis.org

Epilepsy Foundation
4351 Garden City Drive,
Landover, MD 20785
Phone: (800) 332-1000, (301) 459-3700
Web site: www.efa.org

Helen Keller National Center for Deaf/Blind Youths and Adults
111 Middle Neck Road
Sands Point, NY 11050
Phone: (516) 944-8900 (Voice); (516) 944-8637 (TTY)
Fax: (516) 944-7302
Web site: www.hellenkeller.org

Medicaid

Medicaid is a state administered and federally reimbursed program that pays directly for needed medical care for eligible people. An applicant's medical diagnoses, financial history and age are used to determine Medicaid eligibility. For more information contact Social Security Administration at 1 (800) 772-1213, Web site: www.ssa.gov. or contact your local Social Security Office using the Yellow Pages. The Social Security Administration has many pamphlets available which can be requested, including *Benefits For Children With Disabilities* (Pub. No. 05-10026); *Working While Disabled* (Pub. No. 05195) *Supplemental Security Income* (Pub. No. 05-11053). Also see Supplemental Security Income (SSI).

Muscular Dystrophy Association - USA
National Headquarters
3300 E. Sunrise Drive
Tucson, AZ 85718
Phone: (800) 572-1717
E-mail: mda@mdausa.org
Web site: www.mdausa.org

National Association of the Deaf
814 Thayer AvenueSilver Spring, MD 20910-4500
Phone: (301) 587-1788 TTY: (301) 587-1789
Fax: (301) 587-1791
E-mail: NADinfo@nad.org
Web site: http://www.nad.org/

National Association of the Physically Handicapped (NAPH)
Jim Truman, National President, NAPH
754 Staeger St.
Akron, OH 44306-2940
Phone: (330) 724-1994
E-mail:jim@naph.net
Web site: www.naph.net

National Easter Seal Society
230 West Monroe Street, Suite 1800
Chicago, IL 60606
Phone: (800) 221-6827; (312) 726-6200; (312) 726-4258 (TTY)
Fax: (312) 726-1494
E-mail: info@easter-seals.org
Web site: www.easter-seals.org

National Multiple Sclerosis Society
733 Third AvenueNew York, NY 10017
Phone: (800) Fight MS (344-4867)
E-mail: info@nmss.org
Web site: www.nmss.org

National Information Center for Children and Youth with Disabilities (NICHCY)
P.O. Box 1492
Washington, D.C. 20013-1492
Phone: (800) 695-0285 (voice/TTY); (202) 884-8200 (voice/TTY)
Fax: (202) 884-8441
E-mail: nichcy@aed.org
Web site: www.nichcy.org

National Rehabilitation Information Center (NARIC)
1010 Wayne Avenue, Suite 800
Silver Spring, MD 20910
Phone: (800) 346-2742; (301) 562-2400; (301) 495-5626 (TTY)
Fax: (301) 562-2401Web site: www.naric.com

Expanded Information:
Organizations, Programs and Information Centers

Autism Organizations

Autism or Autistic Spectrum Disorder (ASD) is a complex neurological, brain disorder with mild to severe behavioral problems in communicating, responding to the surroundings or interacting with others. The signs, symptoms and the severity of autism vary widely from individual to individual. That is why many physicians and psychologists are calling autism, Autistic Spectrum Disorder (ASD). The diagnosis of autism or ASD is often overlooked until the ages of two to four, when physicians and psychologists carefully observe the child's behavior, especially problems in communication, and impaired social interactions and play with others or alone. If there is trouble determining the diagnosis of autism or ASD by the primary care physician (pediatrician, family physician), psychologist or counselor, be an advocate for your child and seek out a pediatrician specializing in developmental medicine, rehabilitation or pediatric neurology. There is no blood test or brain scan to reliably diagnose autism or ASD. Treatment is based on behavior modification, educational support and sometimes medication. Early diagnosis is most important, with early intervention in years 1-3.

The National Institutes of Health (NIH) report that as many as one in every 500 children have autism or ASD. There are over 500,000 people with autism in the U.S., and autism in children is the third most common developmental disability after cerebral palsy and mental retardation. Symptoms of autism or ASD appear between the ages of one to two years, affecting boys four times more than girls. For more information, consult your pediatrician or family physician and the following organizations:

Asperger Syndrome Coalition of The United States
P.O. Box 49267
Jacksonville, FL 32240-9267
Phone: (904) 745-6741
E-mail: info@asc-us.org
Web site: www.asperger.org

Autism Independent UK
199/201 Blanford Avenue
Kettering, Northants NN169AT
United Kingdom
Phone/Fax: 01536 523274
E-mail: autism@rmplc.co.uk
Web site: www.autismuk.com

Autism National Committee
P.O. Box 6175
N. Plymouth, MA 02362-6175
Phone/Fax: (781) 658-1813
Web site: www.autcom.org

Autism Research Institute
4182 Adams Avenue
San Diego, CA 92116
Phone: (619) 281-7165
Fax: (619) 563-6840
Web site: www.autism.com/autism

Autism Resources
Web site: www.unc.edu/-cory/autism-info

Autism Society of America
7190 Woodmont Ave., Suite 300
Bethesda, MD 20814-3067
Phone: (800) 328-8476; (301) 657-0881
Fax: (301) 657-0869
Web site: www.autism-society.org

Autism Society of Canada
129 Yorkville Ave. #202
Toronto, Ontario CANADA
M5R 1C4
Phone: (416) 922-0302
Fax: (416) 922-1032

Center for Study of Autism
P.O. Box 4538
Salem, OR 97302
Phone/Fax: (503) 363-9110
E-mail: sait@teleport.com
Web site: www.autism.org

MAAP Services, Inc.
P.O. Box 524
Crown Point, IN 46308
Phone: (219) 662-1311
Fax: (219) 662-0638
E-mail: chart@netnitco.net
Web site: www.maapservices.org

National Autism Hotline/Autism
Services Center
605 Ninth St., Prichard Bldg.
P.O. Box 507
Huntington, WV 25710-0507
Phone: (304) 525-8014
Fax: (304) 525-8026

The Autism Network for Hearing
& Visually Impaired Persons
c/o Dolores and Alan Bartel
7510 Oceanfront Ave.
Virginia Beach, VA 23451
Phone: (757) 428-9036
Fax: (757) 428-0019

CAN (Cure Autism Now)
5545 Wilshire Blvd., Ste. 715
Los Angeles, CA 90036
Phone: (888) 8-AUTISM (288476); (323) 549-0500
Fax: (323) 549-0547
E-mail: info@cureautismnow.org
Web site: www.canfoundation.org

Indiana Resource Center for Autism (IRCA)
Indiana Institute on Disability And Community at
Indiana University Bloomington
2853 E. Tenth St.
Bloomington, IN 47408-2696
Phone: (812) 855-6508; (812) 855-9396 (TDD)
Fax: (812) 855-9630
E-mail: prattc@indiana.edu
Web site: www.isdd.indiana.edu/-irca

The National Alliance for Autism Research
99 Wall St.; Research Park
Princeton, NJ 08540
Phone: (888) 777-NAAR (5227); (609) 430-9160
Fax: (609) 430-9163
E-mail: naar@naar.org
Web site: www.naar.org

On-line Asperger's Syndrome
Information and Support (OAS)
E-mail: bkrby@udel.edu
Web site: www.udel.edu/bkirby/asperger

TEACCH
310 Medical School Wing E
University of North Caroline at
Chapel Hill/CB #7180
Chapel Hill, NC 257599-7180
Phone: (919) 966-2174
Fax: (919) 966-4127
E-mail: teacch@unc.edu
Web site: www.teacch.com

Yale Program for Autism, Prader-Willi Syndrome, and Williams Syndrome
Yale Child Study Center
230 S. Frontage Rd.
P.O. Box 207900
New Haven, CT 06520-7900
Phone: (203) 785-7923
Fax: (203) 785-7611
E-mail: devdis.clinic@yale.edu

Cerebral Palsy Organizations

Cerebral palsy (CP): CP is a disorder of body movement, coordination and posture due to a non-progressive injury to the part of the brain called the cerebrum (large area of the brain including the cerebral hemispheres and the basal ganglia). The injury results from very low oxygen (anoxia) occurring from before or during birth up to five years of age. The types of CP are *spastic* (very tight, constant muscle contractions), *dyskinetic* (constant, slow writhing movements of mostly the arms, called choreoathetoid movements), *hypotonic* (very weak), and *mixed forms* of CP, which is a combination.

American Academy for Cerebral Palsy
and Developmental Medicine
Rosemont, IL 60018-4226
Phone: (847) 698-1635
Fax: (847) 823-0536
Web site: www.aacpdm.org

Cerebral Palsy Overseas
6 Dukes Mews
London, WIM 5RB
England
Phone: (0) 71-486-6996
Fax: (0) 71-224-4548

International Cerebral Palsy Society
5A Netherhall Gardens
London NW3 5RN
England
Phone: 01-794-9761

Ontario Federation for Cerebral Palsy
104-1630 Lawrence Avenue West
Toronto, ON, M6L 1C5
CANADA
Phone: (416) 244-9686, Toll-Free (in Canada only): (877) 244-9686
Fax: (416) 244-6543
E-mail: ofcp@ofcp.on.ca
Web site: www.ofcp.on.ca

United Cerebral Palsy Associations, Inc.
1660 L Street, NWSuite 700Washington, DC 20036
Phone: (800) 872-5827, (202) 776-0406, (202) 973-7197 (TDD)
Fax: (202) 776-0414, (202) 776-0416
E-mail: mailto:ucpnatl@ucpa.orgWeb site: www.ucpa.org

Dental Services

**Illinois Foundation of Dentistry for the
Homebound and Handicapped**
211 East Chicago Avenue
Chicago, IL 60611
Phone: (312) 440-8976

Foundation of Dentistry for the Handicapped
New Jersey Dental Association
One Dental Plaza
P.O. Box 6020
North New Brunswick, NJ 08902
Phone: (732)-821-9400
Fax: (732) 821-1082
E-mail: mbelowsky@nfdh.org
Web site: www.nfdh.org

National Foundation of Dentistry for the Handicapped
1800 15th Street
Denver, CO 80202
Phone: (303) 534-5360
Fax: (3030 534-5290
E-mail: Fleviton@nfdh.org
Web site: www.nfdh.org

Nonverbal Learning Disorder (NLD or NVLD)

Nonverbal learning disorder (NLD) is a neurological syndrome, which consists of deficits or difficulties in fine and gross motor skills (such as overall coordination, balance and hand-eye coordination), lack of visual, spatial and organizational skills and poor social skills with difficulties adjusting to non-verbal communication (such as social situations requiring social judgment and social interaction). These deficits may be masked by normal speech and vocabulary development, good rote memory skills especially with auditory retention and early development of reading and spelling skills.

For more information on nonverbal learning disorder, contact the following Web sites.

1. The Nonverbal Learning Disorder Line (NDLline), Web site: www.NLDline.com, maintains a national database to network those parents, professionals and other individuals interested in NLD. The NDLline e-mail is nldline@aol.com. The NLDline information packet, via the Web site, www.nldline.com/infopack1.htm, lists various resources including books, videos, audio tapes, and current in-service seminars and workshops.

2. Nonverbal Learning Disorder On The Web (NDLontheWeb), Web site: www.NLDontheweb.org, provides information about NLD including news, conferences, general information and various resources. Under the Local Resources tab are listed NLD support groups in the United States and Canada as well as summer camps. Their e-mail address is: resources@NLDontheweb.org.

    NDL On The Web also provides extensive links to other related U.S. and Canadian organizations and Web sites for the following:

    a. American Hyperlexia Association (AHA)
    b. American Speech-Language-Hearing Association (ASHA)
    c. Anxiety Disorders Association of America (ADAA)
    d. Anxiety Disorders Education Program of the National Institute of Mental Health
    e. Asperger Syndrome Coalition of the United States, Inc. (ASC – U.S.), for merely called the ASPEN of America, Inc.
    f. Canadian Hyperlexia Assocation
    g. Children and Adults with Attention Deficit/Hyperactivity Disorder (CHADD)

  h. Dyspraxia Foundation
  i. Learning Disabilities On Line (LD OnLine)
  j. National Attention Deficit Disorder Association (ADDA)
  k. National Center for Learning Disabilities (NCLD)
  l. NLDline
  m. Online Asperger Syndrome Information and Support (O.A.S.I.S.)
  n. Tera's NLD Jumpstation: a Resource on Nonverbal Learning Disabilities by an NLD Person.

An excellent reference book on nonverbal learning disorder is:

The Source for Nonverbal Learning Disorders
by Sue Thompson. Copyright © 1997, ISBN 0-7606-0163-1
Publisher: LinguiSystems, Inc.
3110 4th Avenue
East Moline, IL 61244-9700
Phone: (800) PRO-IDEA (776-4332), (800) 933-8331 (TDD)
Fax: (800) 577-4555
E-mail: service@linguisystems.com
Web site: www.linguisystems.com

Nutritional Needs

Administration on Developmental Disabilities
Administration for Children and Families
U.S. Department of Health and Human Services
Mail Stop: HHH 300-F
370 L'Enfant Promenade, S.W.
Washington, D.C. 20447
Phone: (202) 690-6590
Web site: www.acf.dhhs.gov/programs/add

National Dairy Council
C/O Inland Marketing Services
3030 Airport Road
La Crosse, WI 54603
Phone: (800) 426-8271
Fax: (800) 974-6455
Web sites: www.nationaldairycouncil.org, or www.nutritionexplorations.org or www.familyfoodzone.com

National Dairy Council of Canada (NDCC)
221 Laurier Avenue East
Ottawa, Ontario
K1N 6P1Canada
Phone: (613) 238-4116
Fax: (613) 238-6247
Web site: www.ndcc.ca

Food and Nutrition Information Center
National Agricultural Library Building
10301 Baltimore Avenue
Beltsville, MD 20705
Phone: (301) 504-5755
Web site: www.nal.usda.gov/fnic

Parent Advocacy Center for Educational Rights (PACER) Center

National Office:
8161 Normandale Blvd.
Minneapolis, Minnesota 55437
Phone: (952) 838-9000, (952) 838-0190 (TTY),
Toll-free in Greater Minnesota: (800) 537-2237
Fax: (952) 838-0199
E-mail: pacer@pacer.org
Web site: www.pacer.org

*There are parent training and information centers and community groups in the United States that assist parents of infants, toddlers, school-aged children, and young adults with disabilities and the professionals who work with their families. Parent training and information helps parents to participate more effectively with professionals in meeting the educational needs of children and youth with disabilities. To reach the parent center in your state, please contact the technical assistance alliance for parent centers (the Alliance), which coordinates the delivery of technical assistance to the Parent Training and Information Centers and the Community Parent Resource Centers through four regional centers, listed below, located in California, New Hampshire, Texas, and Ohio. **Alliance Coordinating Office:**

PACER Center
8161 Normandale Blvd.
Minneapolis, MN 55437-1044
Phone: (952) 838-9000, (952) 838-0190 (TTY),
Toll free in Minnesota: (800) 537-2237
Fax: (952) 838-0199
E-mail: alliance@taalliance.org
Web site: www.taalliance.org
Contact persons: Paula F. Goldberg, Project Co-Director
Sharman Davis Barrett, Project Co-Director
Sue Folger, Project Co-Director
Dao Xiong, Multicultural Advisor
Jesus Villaseñor, Multicultural Advisor
*This list of federally funded Parent Centers was generated by the Alliance
Coordinating Office at the PACER Center, listed above.*

Northeast Regional Center:
Parent Information Center
P.O. Box 2405
Concord, NH 03302-2405
603-224-7005 voice
603-224-4379 fax
E-mail: picnh@aol.com
Contact Persons:
Judith Raskin, Regional Director,
Mary Trinkley, Technical Assistance Coordinator
Lillye Ramos Spooner, Multicultural TA Coordinator
CT, DE, DC, ME, MD, MA, NH, NJ, NY, PA, Puerto Rico, RI, US VI, VT

Midwest Regional Center: Ohio Coalition for
the Education of Children with Disabilities (OCECD)
Bank One Building
165 West Center Street, Suite 302
Marion, OH 43302-3741
Phone: (740) 382-5452
Fax: (740) 383-6421
E-mail: ocecd@gte.net
Contact Persons:
Margaret Burley, Regional Director
Dena Hook, Technical Assistance Coordinator
Gloria Mitchell, Multicultural TA Coordinator
CO, IL, IA, IN, KS, KY, MI, MN, MO, NE, ND, OH, SD, WI

South Regional Center:
Partners Resource Network, Inc.
1090 Longfellow Drive, Suite B
Beaumont, TX 77706-4819
Phone: (409) 898-4684
Fax: (409) 898-4869
E-mail: txprn@pnx.com
Contact Persons:
Janice S. Meyer, Regional Director
Beverly Elrod-Wilson, Technical Assistance Coordinator
J. Linda Juarez, Multicultural TA Coordinator
AL, AR, FL, GA, LA, MS, NC, OK, SC, TN, TX, VA, WV

West Regional Center:
Matrix Parent Network and Resource Center
94 Galli Drive, Suite C
Novato, CA 94949
Phone: (415) 884-3535
Fax: (415) 884-3555
E-mail: matrix@matrixparents.org
Contact Persons:
Deidre Hayden, Regional Director
Nora Thompson, Technical Assistance Coordinator
Patricia Valdez, Multicultural TA Coordinator
AK, AZ, Department of Defense Dependent Schools (DODDS), CA, HI, ID,
MT, NV, NM, OR, Pacific Jurisdiction, UT, WA, WY

Speech and Communication

Communication Aids
Crestwood Company
6625 North Sidney Place
Milwaukee, WI 53209
Phone: (414) 352-5678
Fax: (414) 352-5679
E-mail: crestcomm@aol.com
Web site: www.communicationaids.com

Enabling Devices
Toys for Special Children
385 Warburton Avenue
Hastings-on-Hudson, NY 10706
Phone: (800) TEC-TOYS (832-8697), (914) 478-0960
Fax: (914) 978-7030
Web site: www.enablingdevices.com

National Institute on Disability and Rehabilitation Research (NIDRR),
(formerly called the National Institute for Handicapped Research)
400 Maryland Avenue, S.W.
Washington, DC 20202-2572
Phone: (202) 205-8134, (202) 205-9433 (TTY), (202) 205-8189 (TTY)
Web site: www.ed.gov/offices/OSERS/NIDRR

National Rehabilitation Information Center (NARIC)
1010 Wayne Avenue, Suite 800
Silver Spring, MD 20910
Phone: (800) 346-2742, (301) 562-2400, (301) 495-5626 (TTY)
Fax: (301) 562-2401
Web site: www.naric.com

Prentke Romich Company
1022 Heyl Road
Wooster, OH 44691
Phone: (800) 262-1984
Fax: (330) 263-4829
Web site: www.prentrom.com

ZYGO Industries, Inc.
P.O. Box 1008
Portland, OR 97207-1008
Phone: (800) 234-6006 (in U.S.A. & Canada), (503) 684-6006
Fax: (503) 684-6011
Web site: www.zygo-usa.com

For further information on national programs and information centers related to speech and communication, please refer to the chapter, "Assistive Technology Devices and Services."

Supplemental Security Income

Supplemental Security Income (SSI) is a federal program that provides income from the federal government to those who are "aged," "blind" or "disabled." Cash benefits are paid on a monthly basis with many states adding additional money to the basic federal rate. The SSI benefits enable an individual with a disability or the family to pay for living expenses and other items not covered by insurance such as co-payments and certain equipment. Beyond the monthly benefit payment, SSI may also entitle the individual to other benefits and services such as Medicaid, food stamps and the payment of Medicare premiums on a state-by-state basis. Eligibility for both SSI and Medicaid is based on financial need. For more information contact the Social Security Administration at 1 (800) 772-1213, Web site: www.ssa.gov. or contact your local Social Security office using the Yellow Pages. The Social Security Administration has many pamphlets available which can be requested, including *Benefits For Children With Disabilities* (Pub. No. 05-10026); *Working While Disabled* (Pub. No. 05195) *Supplemental Security Income* (Pub. No. 05-11053). Also see Supplemental Security Income (SSI).

United States Department of Education

The U.S. Department of Education is an excellent source of information, including pamphlets and copies of the federal laws that can be sent to your home or downloaded on a computer. Call, 1-(800)-USA-LEARN (872- 5327) for the **Information Resource Center of the U.S. Department of Education.**

The home page of the U.S. Department of Education is www.ed.gov. Scroll down to the **Disabilities Education (IDEA)** bulleted item: IDEA stands for Individuals with Disabilities Education Act (IDEA) (Public Law 101-476), formerly known as the Education of Handicapped Children's Act (Public Law 94-142). The Individuals with Disabilities Act (IDEA) now includes the IDEA Amendments of 1997 (Public law 105-17). Under this bulleted item, Disabilities Education Act (IDEA), there are very informative sections such as: What's New, General Information, The Law, IDEA '97 Updates, Letter and Memos and Regulations. You can also order publications, on-line, under the heading "Order Publications On-line". Another number for the U.S. Department of Education is 1-800-421-3481 and their specific Web site address for publications is: www.ed.gov/offices/OCR/ocrpubs.html.

Another important agency sponsored by the U.S. Department of Education is the **Educational Resource Information Center (ERIC),** which can be reached by calling (800)- LET ERIC (538-3742). ERIC will send you information directly to your home. The ERIC Web site is: www.ed.gov/EdRes/EdFed/ERIC.html. ERIC offers parents many brochures that provide tips for becoming more involved in their children's education.

Another excellent source of information is: **ERIC Clearinghouse on Disabilities and Gifted Education and The Council for Exceptional**

Children (CEC). They can also send you specific publications and information on the federal laws.

ERIC Clearinghouse on Disabilities and Gifted Education.
1920 Association Drive
Reston, VA 20191.
Phone: (800) 328-0272, (703) 264-9474
E-mail: ericec@cec.sped.org
Web site: www.ericec.org

The Council for Exceptional Children
1110 North Glebe Road, Suite 300
Arlington, VA 22201-5704
Phone: (888) CEC-SPED, (703) 620-3660, TTY: (text only): (703) 264-9446
Fax: (703) 264-9494
E-mail: service@cec.sped.org
Web site: www.cec.sped.org

Toys

Designed for Children with Disabilities

The following companies offer toys that have been specially designed or adapted for children with disabilities. We recommend that you discuss your child's specific needs and interests with your child's physical or occupational therapist. They often have specific recommendations and current catalogues.

Abledata, Inc.
8630 Fenton Street, Suite 930
Silver Spring, MD 20910
Phone: (800) 227-0216
Fax: (301) 608-8958
E-mail: KABELKNAP@aol.com
Web site: www.abledata.com

AbleNet, Inc,
1081 Tenth Avenue, SE
Minneapolis, MN 55414
Phone: (800) 322-0956 (U.S. and Canada); (612) 379-0956
Fax: (612) 379-9143
E Mail: customerservice@ablenetinc.com
Web site: www.ablenetinc.com

Access Quality Toys
2349 Palomar Avenue
Ventura, CA 93001
Phone: (866) AQTOYS1; (866) 278-6971; (805) 987-2530
E-mail: jo@accessqualitytoys.com
Web site: www.aqtoys.com

Achievement Products, Inc.
PO Box 9033
Canton, OH 44711
Phone: (800) 373-4699
Fax: (800) 453-0222
E-mail: achievepro@aol.com

Battat, Inc.
2 Industrial Boulevard West Circle
PO Box 1264
Plattsburgh, NY 12901
Phone: (800) 247-6144; (518) 562-2200
Fax: (518) 562-2203
In Canada:
8400 Darnley Road
Montreal, QC H4T 1M4
E-mail: sales@battat-toys.com
Web site: www.battat-toys.com

Brio Corporation
N120W18485 Freistadt Road
Germantown, WI 53022
Phone: (888) 274-6869; (262) 250-3240
E-mail: custserv@briotoy.com
Web site: www.briotoy.com

Carolyn's Catalog
1415 57th Avenue West
Bradenton, FL 34207
Phone: (800) 648-2266

Childswork/Childsplay, Inc.
135 DuPont Street
PO Box 760
Plainview, NY 11803-0760
Phone: (800) 962-1141; (516) 349-5520
E-mail: info@childswork.com
Web site: www.childswork.com

Chime Time
Early Childhood Direct
PO Box 369
Landisville, PA 17538
Phone: (800) 784-5717, Customer Service Toll Free: (800) 677-5075
Fax: (800) 219-5253
E-Mail: service@e-c-direct.com
Web site: www.chimetime.com

Crestwood Communication Aids, Inc.
6625 North Sidney Place
Milwaukee, WI 53209-3259
Phone: (414) 352-5678
Fax: (414) 352-5679
E-mail: crestcomm@aol.com
Web site: www.communicationaids.com

Different Roads to Learning, Inc.
Manipulative Toys
12 W. 18th St, Suite 3E
New York, NY 10011
Phone: (800) 853-1057; (212) 604-9637
Fax: (800) 317-9146; (212) 206-9329
E-mail: julie@difflearn.com
Web site: www.difflearn.com

Discovery Toys
PO Box 5023
Livermore, CA 94550
Phone: (800) 426-4777
Web site: www.discoverytoysinc.com

Dragon Fly Toy Company
5725 South 5th Street
Pembina, ND 58271
In Canada:291 Yale Avenue
Winnipeg, MB R3M 0L4
Canada
Phone: (800) 308-2208
Fax: (204) 453-2320
E-mail: dragon@magic.mb.ca
Web site: www.dftoys.com

Eden Toys, LLC
812 Jersey Avenue
Jersey City, NJ 07310
Phone: (800) 443-4275
Web site: www.edentoys.com

Enabling Devices
Toys for Special Children
385 Warburton Avenue
Hastings-on-Hudson, NY 10796
Phone: (800) 832-8697; (914) 478-0960
Fax: (914) 478-7030
Web site: www.enablingdevices.com

Equipment Shop
34 Hartford St.
Bedford, MA 01730
Phone: (800)525-7681; (781) 275-7681
Fax: (781) 275-4094
E-mail: infor@equipmentshop.com
Web site: www.equipmentshop.com

ExploraToy
Division of Educational Insights, Inc.
16941 Keegan Avenue
Carson, CA 90746
Phone: (800) 995-9290
Web site: www.exploratoy.com

Family Resource Services, Inc.
PO Box 1146
Magnolia, AR 71753
Phone: (800) 501-0139; (870) 234-9025;
Fax: (870) 234-9021
E Mail: dorothy@frs-inc.com
Web site: www.frs-inc.com/

Fisher-Price, Inc.
636 Girard Avenue
East Aurora, NY 14052
Phone: (800) 432-5437; (716) 687-3000
Web site: http://www.fisher-price.com

Flaghouse, Inc. - Special Populations
601 Flaghouse Drive
Hasbrouck Heights, NJ 07604-3116
Phone: (800) 793-7900; (201) 288-7600
Fax: (800) 793-7922; (201) 288-7887
E Mail: info@flaghouse.com
Web site: www.flaghouse.com

Fun-Attic, Inc.
3719 Jasmine NE
Grand Rapids, MI 49525
Phone: (877) 293-5315; (616) 559-3642
Fax: (603) 215-2856
E Mail: sales@funattic.com
Web site: www.funattic.com

Funtastic Learning
206 Woodland Road
Hampton, NH 03842
Phone: (800) 722-7375; (603) 926-0071
Fax: (603) 926-5905
E Mail: jay@funtasticlearning.com
Web site: www.funtasticlearning.com

Innovative Products
830 South 48th St.
Grand Forks, ND 58201
Phone: (800) 950-5185
Web site: www.iphope.com

Lakeshore Learning Materials
2695 E. Dominguez St.
P.O. Box 6261
Carson, CA 90749
Phone: (800) 421-5354; (301) 537-8600
Fax: (210) 537-5403
E-mail: lakeshore@lakeshorelearning.com
Web site: www.lakeshorelearning.com

National Lekotek Center
2100 Ridge Avenue
Evanston, IL 60201-2796
Phone: (800) 366-PLAY (Lekotek Toy Resource Helpline); (800) 573-4446
(TTY) (847) 328-0001
Fax: (847) 328-5514
E Mail: lekotek@lekotek.org
Web site: www.lekotek.org

Nintendo of America
4820 150th Ave., NE
Redmond, WA 98052
Phone: (800) 255-3700
The Nintendo Hands-Free Controller
Phone: (800) 422-2602 (Best Resource)
E Mail: nintendo@noa.nintendo.com
Web site: www.nintendo.com

Oppenheim Toy Portfolio
40 East 9th Street, Suite 14M
New York, NY 10003
Phone: (800) 544-8697; (212) 598-0502
Fax: (212) 598-9709
E Mail: stephanie@toyportfolio.com
Web site: www.toyportfolio.com

Parker Brothers, Inc.
PO Box 200Pawtucket, RI 02862
Phone: (800) 327-8264
Web site: www.hasbro.com

Rifton for People with Disabilities
P.O. Box 901
Route 213
Rifton, NY 12471
Phone: (845) 658-8799; (800) 777-4244
Fax: (800) 336-5946
International Fax: (845) 658-8065
Web site: www.communityproducts.com

Sammons Preston, An Ability One Company
Pediatrics Catalog
P.O. Box 5071
Bolingbrook, IL 60440-5071
Phone: (800) 323-5547; (800) 325-1745 (TDD)
Fax: (800) 547-4333
E-mail: sp@sammonspreston.com
Web site: www.sammonspreston.com

S&S Worldwide
PO Box 513
75 Mill St.Colchester, CT 06415-0513
Phone: (800) 243-9232
E Mail: service@snswwide.com
Web site: www.snswwide.com

Tack-Tiles® Braille Systems
PO Box 475Plaistow, NH 03865
Phone: (800) TACK-TILE (822-5845)
U.S. and Canada (603) 382-1748
Fax: (603) 382-1748
E Mail: Braille@tack-tiles.com
Web site: www.tack-tiles.com

Therapeutic Toys, Inc.
P.O. Box 418
Moodus, CT 06469-0418
Phone: (800) 596-9495

TFH (USA) Ltd.
4537 Gibsonia Road
Gibsonia, PA 15044
Phone: (800) 467-6222
Fax: (724) 444-6411
E Mail: tfh@tfhusa.com
Web site: www.tfhusa.com

Toy Manufacturers of America
Guide to Toys for Children Who Are Blind or Visually Impaired
1115 Broadway, Suite 400
New York, NY 10010
Phone: (212) 675-1141
E Mail: info@toy-tma.org
Web site: www.toy-tma.org

Worldwide Games
P.O. Box 513
Colchester, CT 06415-0517
Request the catalog that contains specially designed and adapted board games and activities for recreation and therapy.
Phone: (800) 243-9232, Fax: (800) 566-6678
E-mail: service@ssww.com
Web site: www.ssww.com

Bikes, Wheelchairs, Activity Chairs, Assistance Chairs and Strollers

Designed and Adapted for Children with Disabilities

Bikes

Bicycles, tricycles, hand-cycles, step-operated cycles, tandems and accessories designed and adapted for children with disabilities can be purchased from the following companies:

Equipment Shop
34 Hartford St.
Bedford, MA 01730
Phone: (800)525-7681; (781) 275-7681
Fax: (781) 275-4094
E Mail: infor@equipmentshop.com
Web site: www.equipmentshop.com, click on "Cycles & Accessories"

Frank Mobility Systems, Inc.
Phone: (888) 426-8581
Web site: www.FrankMobility.com
The Duet is the "Go-Anywhere" Wheelchair/Bicycle Tandem, which allows friends and family to go for a ride together. The wheelchair in front separates for use on its own and for transporting. Optional electric motor is available.

Freedom Concepts, Inc.
P.O. Box 45117
RPO Regent
Winnipeg, Manitoba
Canada R2C 5C7
Phone: (800) 661-9915
Fax: (204) 654-1149
E-mail: bikes@freedomconcepts.com
Web site: www.freedomconcepts.com

Haverich Ortho-Sport, Inc.
165 Martell Court
Keene, NH 03431
Phone: (800) 529-9444; (603)358-0438
Fax: (603) 358-0453
E-mail: General information, info@haverich.com
Sales, sales@haverich.com
Service, service@haverich.com
Web site: www.haverich.com

The Love Bike™
P.O. Box 88
Sonoma, CA 95476
Phone: (707) 938-2429
Fax: (707) 938-2459
E Mail: rocky@lovebike.com
Web site: www.lovebike.com

Rock N' Roll Cycle
P.O. Box 1558
Levelland, TX 79336
Phone: (806) 894-5700
Fax: (806) 894-1238
E Mail: funmachines@rocknrollcycles.com
Web site: www.rocknrollcycles.com
Rock N' Roll Cycles are hand or foot powered or a combination of both
hands and feet powering the cycle.

Step'n Go™ Cycles
6 Linden Terrace
Burlington, VT 05401-4928
Phone: (800) 648-7335; (802) 862-2980
Fax: (802) 864-6156
E Mail: info@stepngo.com
Web site: www.stepngo.com
Step 'n Go is a 3-wheel, step-action cycle which eliminates the circular ped-
aling motion and replaces it with an up-and-down stepping action.

Trailmate, Inc.
2359 Trailmate Drive
Sarasota, FL 34243
Phone: (941) 755-5511; (800) 777-1034
Fax: (941) 758-5141; (800) 477-5141
E-mail: info@trailmate.com
Web site: www.trailmate.com

Hand-Cranking Cycles
Angletech
318 N Highway 67
PO Box 1893
Woodland Park, CO 80866-1893
Phone: (800) 793-3038; (719) 687-7475
E-mail: ANGLEZOOM@aol.com
Web site: www.angletechcycles.com

Freedom Ryder Hand Cycles
721 N. Taft Hill Road
Ft Collins, CO 80521
Phone: (800) 991-2790; (970) 221-4290
Fax: (970) 221-4308
E-mail: ack@frii.com
Web site: www.freedomryder.com

Invacare Top End
4501 63rd Circle North
Pinellas Park, FL 33781
Phone: (800) 532-8677; (727) 532-8677
Fax: (727) 522-1007

Invacare Corporation
One Invacare Way
P.O. Box 4028
Elyria, OH 44036-2125
Phone: (800) 333-6900; (444) 329-6000
E-mail via Invacare Web site, below.
Web site: www.invacare.com

Lightning Handcycles
360 Sepulveda Blvd,
Suite 1005
El Segundo, CA 90245
Phone: (888) 426-3292
(310) 821-0259
Fax: (310) 335-1543
E-mail: information@handcycle.com
Web site: www.handcycle.com

Wheelchairs, Activity Chairs and Assistance Chairs

Wheelchairs designed and adapted for children with disabilities can be purchased from the following companies:

Columbia Medical Manufacturing Corp.
Dept. D2
P.O. Box 633
Pacific Palisades, CA 90272
Phone: 1-800-454-6612
Fax: (310) 305-1718
E Mail: CMedOnline@aol.com
Web site: www.ColumbiaMedical.com
Offers adaptive devices for toileting, bathing and transporting children.

Deming Design, Inc.
141 W. Pineestead Rd.
Pensacola, FL 32503
Phone: (850) 478-5765
Fax: (850) 476-3361
E Mail: kmdeming@aol.com
Web site: www.beachwheelchair.com
De-Bug wheelchairs allow access to nature, including the beaches and trails in the woods. Special features and modifications include stainless steel frame and waterproof fabric construction, separate tires for pool use, sun umbrella, fishing pole holder, drink holder, custom headrest and a self-propulsion feature.

Duralife, Inc.
195 Phillips Park Drive
South Williamsport, PA 17702, USA
Phone: 1-800-443-5433
Fax: (570) 323-9762
E Mail: duralife@aol.com
Web site: www.duralife-usa.com
In Canada:
Phone: (519) 271-6799
Fax: (519) 271-6768
E-mail slhs@strat.net
Supplier of the "Adjustable-Bath Chair" and Pediatric Shower/Commode Chairs.

Innovative Products, Inc.
830 South 48th Street
Grand Forks, North Dakota 58201 USA
Phone: 1-800-950-5185
Web site: www.iphope.com
Innovative Products manufactures mobility devices that assist children with severe physical disabilities, such as cerebral palsy and spina bifida, including standing frames within the Go-Bot, Mini Go-Bot, and Gait Trainerplus the low-riding recreational vehicle called the Go-Kart.

The Landeez All-Terrain Wheelchair
From Natural Access
Phone: (800) 411-7789
Outside the U.S.A.: (310) 392-9864
Web site: www.landeez.com
The Landeez all-terrain and beach wheelchair has been designed to roll on sand, snow and gravel using soft plastic pneumatic tires, which absorb road shock to provide a comfortable ride.

Sammons Preston, An Ability One Company
4 Sammons Court
Bollingbrook, IL 60440
Phone: 1-800-323-5547
In Canada: 1-800-665-9200
Fax: 1-800-547-4333
E Mail: sp@sammonspreston.com
Web site: www.sammonspreston.com
Suppliers of the "Leckey Bath Chair" and other adaptive devices for standing, sitting, toilet use and showering.

Snug Seat, Inc.
P.O. Box 1739
Matthews, NC 28106-1739
Phone: 1-800-336-7684
Fax: (704) 882-0751
E Mail: info@snugseat.com
Web site: snugseat.com
The Snug Seat Company produces a variety of wheelchairs, rehabilitation strollers, bike trailers, snow ski buggies, various car seats with options and activity chairs with multiple adjustments for depth, height and angle.

Strollers

Strollers designed and adapted for children with disabilities can be purchased from the following companies:

Baby Jogger
P.O. Box 2189
Yakima, WA 98907
Phone: (800) 241-1848; (509) 457-0925
Fax: (509) 453-7732
Web site: www.babyjogger.com
The Baby Jogger Company advertises the following features: rolls easily over any terrain, folds easily, has a 5-point harness and quick-release wheels. The Baby Jogger Company also offers to custom fit a stroller for your child that has special needs.

CycleTote Corporation
517 No.Link Ln.
Ft. Collins, CO 80524
Phone: (800) 747-2407; (970) 482-2401
Fax: (970) 482-2402
Web site: www.cycletote.com
CycleTote strollers and bicycle trailer can be modified for children with special needs using various available seats, the 5-point harness plus the company offers customizing.

Sports Therapy

General Information on Sports Therapy

Sports therapy is the enjoyment of a sport, which results in improvements in gross motor function as measured in the clinic by licensed physical and occupational therapists or physicians. Sports therapy is the active participation of a child or an adult in a sport as a form of therapy with specially trained instructors and volunteers using adaptive equipment and assisting the individual to have fun. Sports therapy used in the early years of development may help children with physical disabilities such as cerebral palsy (CP) as well as lower the medical bills and personal expenses to families and society. Examples of Sports therapies include horseback riding, skiing (downhill and cross-country skiing), swimming, baseball, skating (ice and in-line skating), hockey, hiking, bicycling, dancing, tennis, hiking with an assistant or a dog trained as a service animal (see chapter 15 on Service Dogs).

Benefits of sports therapy may include:

(1) Life-long active participation in one's own rehabilitation
(2) Better participation in traditional physical/occupational therapy
(3) High self-esteem while having fun
(4) Inclusion in activities with family and friends
(5) Interaction and acceptance by peers
(6) Actual therapy without emphasizing the negative term "therapeutic" and
(7) Improved self-identity as a *horseback rider, skier,* or *swimmer* with high motivation, enthusiasm and pride.

Horseback Riding Therapy

Horseback riding therapy throughout North America has become very popular. There are over 600 North American Riding for the Handicapped Association (NARHA) horseback riding centers in the U.S. and Canada. There are also hundreds of other horseback riding centers all serving children with various neurological disabilities.

Horseback riding therapy uses a team approach with an instructor and a side-walker performing the sports therapy under safe horseback riding conditions. The warmth of the trained horse through the horse blanket plus the slow, controlled walk of the horse may help relax spastic muscles in children with cerebral palsy. Horseback riding directly on a horse blanket or using a saddle also provides the rider with the same pelvic movements seen in normal walking. The movements of the horse may help the rider by stretching and stimulating the muscles for balance, posture and walking.

Physicians and physical and occupational therapists in Western New York State in collaboration with physicians and physiotherapists in Ontario, Canada have documented that horseback riding actually improves total gross motor function in children with cerebral palsy. After completing a summer and fall season (twelve weeks) of horseback riding, lasting physical benefits in walking, running and jumping are seen in these children with cerebral palsy. These children were evaluated with "Sports Check-ups," which were enjoyable one-hour evaluations done every six weeks before, during and after the horseback riding season, spring through fall. Horseback riding was done at nearby therapeutic horseback riding centers in Western New York. Physicians and therapists concluded that horseback riding improves gross motor function, especially walking running and jumping, reducing gross motor disability in children with cerebral palsy. Horseback riding is fun, safe and has now been medically recommended as sports therapy for the rehabilitation of children having cerebral palsy. This research was presented at the Annual Meeting of the American Academy for Cerebral Palsy & Developmental Medicine (AACPDM), September 22, 2000. This research was subsequently published in the peer-reviewed, scientific medical literature: Sterba, JA, BT Rogers, AP France, DA Vokes. Horseback riding in children with cerebral palsy: effects on gross motor function. *Developmental Medicine & Child Neurology* 2002, 44: 301-308.

Horseback Riding Therapy Programs in the U.S. and Canada

The first therapeutic riding program in North America was established in Toronto, Ontario in 1965 as the Community Association for Riding for the Disabled (CARD). At this same time, another therapeutic riding program began in Windsor, Ontario under the direction of the Canadian Red Cross. Two years later in the United States, the National Foundation for Happy Horsemanship for the Handicapped (HHFTH) became established in 1967 in Malvern, Pennsylvania.

The North American Riding for the Handicapped Association (NARHA) was founded in 1969 to support riders from both the United States and Canada. In 1970, the first center dedicated only for therapeutic horseback riding was built in Augusta, Michigan, known as the Cheff Center for the Handicapped.

The demand for horseback riding therapy throughout North America has led to the current operation of 600 NARHA accredited horseback riding centers serving an estimated 35,000 individuals, primarily children having developmental delay and various neurological disabilities in the United States and Canada. A majority of the time, these children participate in recreational, horseback riding therapy programs on a weekly basis. For further information, including location of a horseback-riding facility, contact NARHA. See chapter 13, Directory of Sports Therapy and Recreational Programs in U.S. and Canada.

Approximately 10 percent of the time, horseback-riding therapy is conducted as hippotherapy by a licensed, healthcare professional, such as a physical, occupational or speech therapist. The NARHA Special Interest Section, American Hippotherapy Association, defines *hippotherapy*. *Hippotherapy*, which is derived from the Greek word, *hippos*, meaning horse, is a form of treatment performed by healthcare professionals in which the horse is used as a therapeutic intervention.

For more information in hippotherapy, contact the American Hippotherapy Association via the NARHA address in chapter 13, Directory of Sports Therapy and Recreational Programs in U.S. and Canada. Also see appendices B and C for examples of horseback riding therapy programs and other sports therapy and recreational programs in Western New York State.

Adaptive Downhill Skiing Therapy

In the last sixty years, adaptive downhill skiing for children and adults with disabilities has expanded internationally, especially in the past thirty years across the United States and Canada. Adaptive downhill skiing is very enjoyable and it is safe. Adaptive downhill skiing uses a team approach with ski instructors trained in adaptive skiing working closely with other skiing assistants and volunteers. Often, ski instructors receive direct input from the skier's physical or occupational therapist. By controlling the skier with tethers and special adaptive skiing devices, skiing may help as a form of therapy by stimulating the developing nervous system as well as stretching and strengthening muscles controlling balance and posture. The primary movements during skiing are also thought to help children and adults to learn how to walk. Adaptive downhill skiing may help to relax spastic muscles and it may also help to improve posture, balance, strength and coordination in children and adults with cerebral palsy.

For more information on adaptive downhill skiing therapy, see chapter 13, Directory of Sports Therapy and Recreational Programs in U.S. and Canada. Also see appendices B and C for examples of adaptive and cross-country skiing therapy programs and other sports therapy and recreational programs in Western New York State.

Swimming or Aquatic Therapy

Swimming therapy, also called aquatic therapy, uses a team approach with a physical or occupational therapist or certified swimming instructor performing the therapy in the shallow end of a warm (92° – 95°F) swimming pool. The water's buoyancy counteracts gravity, supports the individual and allows for a greater number of swimming exercises compared to land-based therapy. The effect of immersion and the warmth of the water, near body temperature, also allow for greater relaxation and range of motion than on dry land. Benefits of aquatic therapy may include:

• Increasing or maintaining flexibility and muscle strength
• Pain reduction
• Improved cardiovascular endurance and aerobic fitness
• Decreasing abnormal tone/spasticity/rigidity

- Improved coordination, balance reactions, head control, trunk stability and posture
- Improved respiration and circulation
- Improved perception, spatial awareness and motivation
- Improved ambulation and functional transfers
- Decreased depression
- Improved self-esteem and socialization.

For more information, contact local physical and occupational therapy offices or the local children's hospital physical and occupational therapy department.

For more information on aquatic therapy programs, see chapter 13, Directory of Sports Therapy and Recreational Programs in U.S. and Canada. Also see appendices B and C for examples of aquatic therapy programs and other sports therapy and recreational programs in Western New York State.

Ice-Skating Therapy

Ice-skating therapy has been reported to physically improve balance, coordination, muscle strength, and endurance. In addition, ice-skating therapy may allow improvements in independence, confidence, stamina, self-esteem, pride and satisfaction. By using special equipment such as adapted walkers and skates designed to fit over ankle braces, children and adults learn how to enjoy the freedom and self-expression of ice-skating with some assistance from dedicated, trained volunteers and skating instructors.

For more information on ice-skating therapy programs, contact:

**Skating Association for the Blind and
Handicapped (SABAH) National, Inc.**
1200 East & West Road
West Seneca, NY 14224
Telephone: (716) 675-SABA (7222)
Fax: (716) 675-7223
E-mail: sabah@sabahinc.org
Web site: www.sabahinc.org.

See chapter 13, Directory of Sports Therapy and Recreational Programs in U.S. and Canada. Also see appendices B and C for examples of ice-skating therapy programs and other sports therapy and recreational programs in Western New York State.

Dance Therapy

By combining music and dance instruction, dance therapy provides the student cognitive, emotional, social and physical development to both ambulatory and non-ambulatory children. The American Dance Therapy Association (ADTA) works to establish and maintain high standards of professional education and competence in the field of dance/movement therapy. The ADTA includes information on dance therapy, membership, upcoming conferences, publications, education, credentials, and research.

ADTA National Office.
Business Hours: 8:30 AM-4:00 PM EST
Phone: (410) 997-4040
Fax: (4l0) 997-4048
E-mail: info@adta.org
Web site: http://www.adta.org

Recreational Programs

M any enjoyable local recreation programs are available through your parks and recreation department for those with disabilities, including:

1. *Activities:* music, dance, arts, crafts, pottery, nature programs, hiking, creative theater and dramatics, games, physical fitness programs, field trips, parks with specially designed playgrounds with good accessibility, day camps and physical fitness programs, bike riding with adapted bicycles or tricycles, photography,
2. *Sports:* Seasonal team sports or sports clinics for baseball, softball, basketball, tennis, soccer, golf, floor hockey, field hockey, ice hockey, arena ice-skating, soccer, flag and tackle football, racquetball, bowling, billiards (pool), table tennis (Ping-Pong).
3. *Adapted Aquatics:* swimming instruction, water games, and aquatic shows.
4. *Outdoor Adventures:* canoeing, boating, sailing, water skiing, fishing, camping, archery, backpacking, horseback riding, cross-country skiing, sledding, tobogganing, outdoor ice-skating, orienteering and rappelling. Some activities require high-skill level.
5. *Social and Special Events:* Dances, clubs, banquets, parties, holiday events, movie-going or restaurant dining.
6. *Camps:* There are camps that meet the many needs of their campers, including: wheel-chair-accessible swimming programs, adaptive sports (sports therapy) and recreational programs, on-site nurses experienced in your child's disabilities, and specially trained counselors to meet your child's physical and emotional needs such as homesickness, eating habits, sleeping habits,

hygiene special needs and getting along with other children in the cabin and at camp. Inquire if the American Camping Association (ACA) accredits the particular camp, and if the "ACA standards for persons with special needs" are also met. Also inquire if your child's specific needs would be met by qualified counselors that are at least 18 years old, with no more than three campers with disabilities per counselor. Often, financial assistance is available due to a growing public awareness and support by donations, grants and state and federal public assistance programs.

Start looking for a camp by contacting your town or city's parks and recreation department. Speak directly to the parks and recreation director about your child's interests and needs and the available sports programs. Often, the director is most supportive and will refer a family to the key person or therapist in charge of various sports therapy and recreational programs.

The physical and occupational therapy departments from the closest children's hospital or near by community hospital often are aware of the local day camps and overnight camps which serve the needs of children with disabilities. Easter Seals offers camps for children with disabilities throughout the United States. Contact Easter Seals headquarters in Chicago, phone: (800) 221-6827, to request specific information for your state for the camps closest to you. The Easter Seals Web site is http://www.easter-seals.org. The American Camping Association Web site is: http://wwwACAcamps.org and their phone numbers are (800) 428-CAMP (2267) and Fax: (765)342-2065. The Epilepsy Foundation affiliates can suggest programs for summer camping and family retreat programs. You can contact them at http://www.efa.org and their phone number is (800) 332-4050. Some United Cerebral Palsy affiliates can offer camping programs. Contact them at http://www.ucpa.org/ or call them at (800) 872-5827. Muscular Dystrophy Association supports almost 90 summer camps throughout the country. Contact them at http://www.mdausa.org or call them at (800) 572-1717. Special Touch Ministry, Inc. is a Christian camp. Contact them at P.O. Box 25, Waupaca, WI 54981 and their phone number is (715) 258-2713, E-mail: ministry@specialtouch.org, Web site:

http://www.specialtouch.org. Also, see appendix C for examples of camps and other recreational programs in Western New York State.

7. *Special Olympics*
   What is the Special Olympics Organization?
   Special Olympics is an international organization dedicated to empowering individuals with mental and physical disabilities to become physically fit, productive and respected members of society through sports training and competition. Special Olympics offers children and adults with mental and physical disabilities year-round training and competition in twenty-six Olympic-type summer and winter sports.
   The Special Olympics Motto: "Let me win. But if I cannot win, let me be brave in the attempt."
   The Special Olympics website will direct you to your local organization to register. Web site: www.specialolympics.org

8. *Navy Run Jump 'n' Throw (RJT) Program*
   5021 Oakcrest Drive
   Fairfax, VA 22030
   Phone: (800) 539-7057
   E-mail: NavyRJT@yahoo.com
   Web site: www.runjumpnthrow.org
   The program basis is simple, utilizing the basic elements of sport, movement, fun, competition and a sense of accomplishment. Through the Run Jump 'n' Throw Program, children with disabilities can learn skills from inclusion with their able-bodied friends and the support of their instructors.

Books on Recreation and Physical Education Programs

1. Kennedy, Dan W., Ralph W. Smith and David R. Austin. *SPECIAL RECREATION: Opportunities for Persons with Disabilities, Second Edition.* Wm. C. Brown Publishers, Dubuque, IA, 1987.
2. Block, Martin E. *A Teacher's Guide to Including Students with Disabilities in General Physical Education, Second Edition.* Paul H. Brooks Publishing, Co., Baltimore, MD, 2000.

Directory of Sports Therapy and Recreational Programs in the U.S. and Canada

- Adaptive Downhill Skiing Therapy
- Basketball
- Billiards
- Bowling
- Camping and Outdoor Activities
- Canoeing
- Craft Aids
- Fishing
- Flying
- Football
- Golf
- Handcycling
- Hockey and Sled or Sledge Hockey
- Horseback Riding Therapy
- Ice Skating
- Quad Rugby
- Rowing
- Sailing
- SCUBA Diving
- Shooting and Archery
- Softball
- Swimming
- Table Tennis
- Tennis
- Water Skiing
- Weightlifting
- General Exercise Equipment
- General Sports and Recreation Organizations

Adaptive Downhill Skiing Therapy Programs in the U.S. and Canada

The Adaptive Sports Center of Crested Butte
PO Box 1639
Crested Butte, CO 81224
Phone: (970) 349-2296
Fax: (970) 349-4950
E-mail: asc1@rmi.net
Web site: www.adaptivesports.org

American Blind Skiing Foundation (ABSF)
610 S. William St.
Mt. Prospect, IL 60056
Phone: (847) 255-1739
Web site: www.absf.org

Breckenridge Outdoor Education Center (BOEC) Adaptive Ski Program
P.O. Box 697
Breckenridge, CO 80424
Phone: (800) 303-BOEC (2632); (970) 453-6422
Fax: (970) 453-4676
E-mail: skiprog@boec.org
Web site: www.boec.org

Canadian Association for Disabled Skiing (CADS)
P.O. Box 307
Kimberly, BC V1A 2Y9
Phone: (250) 427-7712
Contact: Jerry Johnston, Director
E-mail: cads@rockies.net
Web site: www.disabledskiing.ca

Canadian Association for Disabled Skiing (CADS), Alpine Technical Committee
The CADS Alpine Technical Committee is comprised of qualified volunteer ski professionals throughout Canada who have designed adaptive ski equipment and developed teaching methods to assist people with disabilities to ski. The Alpine Technical Committee has produced a teaching manual, "Skiing Methodology for Persons with a Disability," which is available through CADS. The following people serve on the CADS Alpine Technical Committee throughout Canada. For further information, see the CADS Web site: www.disabledskiing.ca or contact Mr. Jerry Johnston, Director CADS, E-mail: cads@rockies.net.

CADS Alpine Technical Committee

Glen Suyama (Board Liaison)
35 Chatham St.
Hamilton ON. L8P 2B3
Phone: (905) 523-7905
E Mail: suyamag@haltonbe.on.ca

Kim Atkins (Chairperson)
115 Silverhill Way NW
Calgary, AB T3B 4K7
Phone: (403) 288-3480
E-mail: katkins@canem.com

Bradford Nip
Box 456
Marysville, BC V0B 1Z0
Phone: (250) 427-7575

Tommy Chevrette
1046 De L'Avenir
Ancienne Lorette, QC G2E 3R2
Phone: (418) 877-4766
Fax: (418) 877-0186
E-mail: tomche@globetrotter.net

Jimmy Colligan
355 Des Epinettes
Val Morin, QC J0T 2R0
Phone: (819) 322-6073

Bob Vickers
180 Scenic Ridge Cr., NW.
Calgary AB. T3L 1V7
Phone: (403) 239-9370
E-mail: aitken@telusplanet.net

Elton Irwin
425 Des Bourgeons
Ste Adele, QC J8B 2E9
Phone: (514) 229-4698

Gord Layhew
3215 Pinemeadow Dr
Burlington, ON L7M 2N6
Phone: (905) 336-0226
E-mail gvlayhew@bserv.com

Paul-Emile Hamel
6 Butternut Box 57 RR2
Wakefield QC. J0X 3G0
Phone: (819) 459-2444
Fax: (819) 459-1913
E-mail: Joanne.hamell2@sympatico.ca

Mike Phelps
Box 1591
Vernon B.C. V1T 8CT
Phone: (250) 558-4549
E-mail: phelps_m@yahoo.coml

Clay Dawdy
31 Kimini Dr.
Stittsville ON. K23 1S6
E-mail: cdawdy@aol.com

Disabled Sports USA (DSUSA)
Kirk Bauer, Executive Director
451 Hungerford Dr.
Suite 100
Rockville, MD 20850
Telephone: (301) 217-0960, TDD: (301) 217-0963
Fax: (301) 217-0968
Web site: www.dsusa.com

National Ability Center (NAC)
P.O. Box 682799
Park City, UT 84068-2799
Telephone: (435) 649-3991
Fax: (435) 658-3992
E-mail: nac@xmission.com
Web site: www.nationalabilitycenter.org

National Sports Center for the Disabled (NSCD)
P.O. Box 1290
Winter Park, CO 80482
Phone: (303) 293-5711 (Denver), (970) 726-1540 (Winter Park)
Fax: (970) 726-4112
E-mail: info@nscd.org
Web site: www.nscd.org

New England Handicapped Sports Association
P.O. Box 2135
Mt. Sunapee, NH 03255-2135
Phone: (800) 628-4484; (603) 763-9158
E-mail: nehsa@sugar-river.net
Web site: www.nehsa.org

Ontario Track 3 Association, (for children 6-19, only)
P.O. Box 67, Station D
Toronto, Ontario M9A 4X1
Phone: (416) 233-3872
E-mail: track3@idirect.com
Web site: www.track3.org

Professional Ski Instructors of America,
(PSIA): Eastern Division, Adaptive
Gwen Allard, Adaptive PSIA Examiner
Ski Windham Ski Resort
2860 Rotary Drive
C.D. Lane Road
Windham, NY 12429
Phone: (518) 734-5070
E-mail: asfwindham@aol.com
Web site: www.wdski.org

Ski for Light
5 McAuliffe Dr.
North Brunswick, NJ 08902
Phone: (609) 520-8079
E-mail: acooke@rfbd.org
Web site: www.sfl.org
* A program of cross-country skiing benefiting blind, visually-impaired, and
mobility-impaired individuals and their guides

U.S. Ski and Snowboard Association (USSA) Disabled Ski Team
P.O. Box 100
Park City, UT 84060
Phone: (435) 649-9090
Fax: (435) 649-3613
E-mail: info@ussa.org
Web site: www.usskiteam.com or www.ussa.org
Contact: Debra, Phone: (207) 236-6273

Windham Ski Resort
Adaptive Sports Foundation
C.D. Lane Road
Windham, NY 12429
Phone: (518) 734-5070
Contact: Gwen Allard, Director
E-mail: epiaw@aol.com
Web site: www.wdski.org

Wintergreen Adaptive Skiing
Wintergreen, VA
E-mail: info@skiwas.org
Web site: www.skiwas.org/prog.html

Skiing Accessories: Nordic (Cross-Country) and Alpine (Downhill) Sit-Skis, Mono-Skis, Bi-Skis, Ski Bras, Outriggers, Bibs and other Adaptive Ski Equipment and Clothing

XC Glider Hall's Wheels
PO Box 784
Cambridge, MA 02238
Phone: (800) 628-7956 (617) 628-7955
Supplies: Nordic Sit-Ski

Mogul Master AT's Freedom Factory
Rt 5 Box 50734
Winnsboro, TX 75494
Phone: (903) 629-3945
Fax: (903) 629-3946
E-mail: freefact@peoplescom.net
Supplies: Mono-Skis

Shadow Rehabilitation Equip. Assn.
8030 S Willow St Unit 4
Manchester, NH 03103
Phone: (603) 645-5200
Supplies: Mono-Skis

Yetti Radventure, Inc.
20755 SW 238th Pl
Sherwood, OR 97140
Phone: (503) 628-2895
Fax: (503) 628-0517
Supplies: Mono-Skis

Grove Innovations
120 W Church Box 185
Centre Hall, PA 16828
Phone: (814) 364-2677
Supplies: Mono-Skis

Strange R+D
P.O. 2247
Banff, Alberta
TOL OCO
CANADA
Phone: (403) 762-5003
Fax: (403) 762-5860
E-mail: strange@telusplanet.net
Supplies: Mono and Bi-Skis

ISOSKI
1046, de l'Avenir
Ancienne-Lorette
Québec, Canada
G2E 3R2
Phone: (418) 877-4766
Fax: (418) 877-0186
E-mail: evalpep@evaluation-pep.qc.ca

Skistar Technologies
PO Box 7461
Tahoe City, CA 96145
Phone: (916) 581-2441
Supplies: Bi-Skis

Mountain Man Bi Ski
FFS Dual Ski
720 Front Street
Bozeman, MT 59715
Phone: (406) 587-0310
Fax: (406) 585-5513
Supplies: Bi-Skis

Spokes N Motion Bi Ski
2225 S Platte River Drive W
Denver, CO 80223
Phone: (303) 922-0605
Fax: (303) 922-7943
E-mail: info@spokesnmotion.com
Supplies: Mono and Bi-Skis, Outriggers, other skiing accessories

Ski Eze-Bras
4401 Devonshire
Lansing, MI 48910
Phone: (517) 882-4608
Supplies: Ski Bras (a device to keep skis together at tips)

Ski Doctor: Shockshaft
609 Munroe St
Sacramento, CA 95825
Phone: (916) 488-5398
Supplies: Outriggers

LaCome, Inc
PO Box 1026
Questa, NM 87556
Phone: (505) 586-0356
Supplies: Outriggers

Reliable Racing Supply
643 Upper Glen Street
Queensbury, NY 12804-2014
Phone: (800) 274-6815
Supplies: Bibs

Vulpine Outerwear Adaptive Apparel and Equipment
Kevin Kinney
4337 Tioga Street
Duluth, MN 55804
Phone: (218) 525-9836
Fax: (218) 525-9836
E-mail: info@vulpineadaptive.com
Web site: www.vulpineadaptive.com
Supplies: Adaptive Outdoor Clothing

Basketball
Canadian Wheelchair Basketball Association (CWBA)
2781 Lancaster Road
Ottawa, ON K1B 1A7
CANADA
Phone: (613) 260-1296
Fax: (613) 260-1456
Web site: www.cwba.ca

General International Wheelchair Basketball Federation
Bob Robert J. Szyman, Ph.D. Secretary
5142 Ville Maria Lane
Hazelwood, MO 63042-1646
Phone: (314) 209-9006
Fax: (314) 739-6688
Web site: www.iwbf.org

National Wheelchair Basketball Association (NWBA)
110 Seaton Building
University of Kentucky
Lexington, KY 40506
Web site: http://www.nwba.org/index2.html, click on "Youth"

Basketball Accessories: Sport Wheelchairs

Allegro Medical
Phone: (800) 861-3211
E-mail: Sales@AllegroMedical.com
Web site: www.allegromedical.com
Supplies: Sport Wheelchairs

Billiards

National Wheelchair Pool Players Association
Michigan Office
30872 Puritan
Livonia, Michigan 48154
Phone: (734) 422-2124
E-mail: deadstrok1@aol.com
Web site: www.nwpainc.com

Billiards Accessories: Rollers, Cue Guides, Extend-A-Bridge

California Office
9651 Halekulani Drive
Garden Grove, California 92841
Phone: (714) 636-3371
E-mail: deadstrok1@aol.com
Web site:: www.nwpainc.com
Supplies: Rollers, Cue Guides, Extend-A-Bridge

Bowling

American Wheelchair Bowling Association (AWBA)
6264 North Andrews Ave.
Ft. Lauderdale, FL 33309
Phone/Fax: (954) 491-2886
E-mail for George H. Snyder, Executive Secretary/Treasurer: george@awba.org
Web site: http://www.awba.org

Bowling Accessories: Ball Holder Ramp, Bowling Ball Ramp, Ball Pusher, Handle Grip Bowling Ball and other Bowling Equipment

Access to Recreation, Inc.
8 Sandra Court
Newbury Park, CA 91320
Phone: (800) 634-4351
E-mail: dkrebs@gte.net
Web site: http://www.accesstr.com
Supplies: Various Bowling Accessories listed above

Briggs Corporation
7300 Westown Parkway
West Des Moines, IA 50266
Phone: (800) 247-2343
Web site: http://www.briggscorp.com
Supplies: Various Bowling Accessories listed above

Sportime Corporation
1 Sportime Way
Atlanta, GA 30340
Phone: (800) 444-5700
Web site: http://www.sportime.com, and click on "abilitations"
Supplies: Various Bowling Accessories listed above

Flaghouse, Inc.
601 Flaghouse Dr.
Hasbrouck Heights, NJ 07604
Phone: (800) 793-7900
Web site: www.flaghouse.com
Supplies: Various Bowling Accessories listed above

Maddak, Inc.,
6 Industrial Rd.
Pequannock, NJ 07440
Phone: (800) 443-4926
Web site: www.maddak.com
Supplies: Various Bowling Accessories listed above

Camping and Outdoor Activities

American Camping Association
5000 State Road, 67 N.
Martinsville, IN 46151-7902
Phone: (800) 428-2267; (765) 342-8456
Fax: (765) 342-2065
E-mail: bookstore@aca-camps.org
Web site: www.acacamps.org

Boy Scouts of America
1325 W. Walnut Hill Ln.
Irving, TX 75038
Phone: (972) 580-2000
Fax: (972) 580-2502
Web site: www.bsa.scouting.org

Breckenridge Outdoor Education Center (BOEC)
P.O. Box 697
Breckenridge, CO 80424
Phone: (800) 383-2632; (970) 453-6422
Fax: (970) 453-4676
E-mail: boec@boec.org
Web site: www.boec.org

Cooperative Wilderness Outdoor Group
(C.W.HOG)
P.O. Box 8128
Pocatello, ID 83209
Phone: (208) 282-3912
Fax: (208) 236-4600
E-mail: branjeff@isu.edu
Web site: www.isu.edu/cwhog/

Girl Scouts of the USA
Membership and Program Group
420 5th Avenue
New York, NY 10018
Phone: (800) 223-0624; (212) 852-8000
Web site: www.gsusa.org

SPLORE Accessible Outdoor Adventures
880 East 3375 South
Salt Lake City, UT 84106
Phone: (801) 484-4128
Fax: (801) 484-4177
E-mail: splore@splore.org
Web site: www.splore.org

VISIONS/Vacation Camp for the Blind
500 Greenwich St., 3rd Fl.
New York, NY 10013-1354
Phone: (212) 625-1616
Fax: (212) 219-4078
E-mail: info@visionsvcb.org
Web site: www.visionsvcb.org

Voyageur Outward Bound School
101 E. Chapman St.
Ely, MN 556731
Phone: (800) 321-4453; (218) 365-7790
Fax: (218) 365-7079
E-mail: vobs@vobs.com
Web site: www.vobs.com

Wilderness Inquiry
808 14th Avenue SE
Minneapolis, MN 55414-1516
Phone: (800) 728-0719 (voice/TDD); (612) 676-9400 (voice/TDD)
Fax: (612) 676-9401
E-mail: info@wildernessinquiry.org
Web site: www.wildernessinquiry.org

Wilderness On Wheels Foundation
3131 S. Vaughn Way, #305
Aurora, CO 80014
Phone: (303) 751-3959
E-mail: wow@coloradopros.com
Web site: www.wildernesonwheels.org

Canoeing

American Canoe Association
7432 Alban Station Blvd.
Ste B-232
Springfield, VA 22150
Phone: (703) 451-0141
Fax: (703) 451-2245
E-mail: acadirect@aol.com
Web site: www.aca-paddler.org

Canoeing Accessories: Boats built for people with disabilities, Cuffs and Various Flotation Devices

Sammons Preston, An Ability One Company
General Catalog, Rehab Supplies
P.O. Box 5071
Bolingbrook, IL 60440-5071
Phone: (800) 323-5547; (800) 325-1745 (TDD)
Fax: (800) 547-4333
E-mail: sp@sammonspreston.com
Web site: www.sammonspreston.com
Supplies: Various flotation devices

Phoenix Products
207 N. Broadway
P. O. Box 109
Berea, KY 40403
Phone: (800) 354-0190
Supplies: Adaptable Boats

Access to Recreation
8 Sandra Court
Newbury Park, CA 91320
Phone: (800) 634-4351
E-mail: dkrebs@gte.net
Web site: www.accesstr.com
Supplies: Grasping Cuffs, and Flotation Devices for Water Sports

Craft Aids: Needle Threaders, Embroidery Hoops, Knitting Aids, Needle Holders

Access to Recreation
8 Sandra Court
Newbury Park, CA 91320
Phone: (800) 634-4351
E-mail: dkrebs@gte.net
Web site: www.accesstr.com
Supplies: Needle Threaders and other accessories as listed above

Sammons Preston, An Ability One Company
General Catalog, Rehab Supplies
P.O. Box 5071
Bolingbrook, IL 60440-5071
Phone: (800) 323-5547; (800) 325-1745 (TDD)
Fax: (800) 547-4333
E-mail: sp@sammonspreston.com
Web site: www.sammonspreston.com
Supplies: Needle Threaders and other accessories as listed above

Fishing

HandiCAPABLE Guide Service.Inc.
P.O. Box 222
Gilbertsville, KY 42044-0222
Phone: (270) 362-0970
Fax: (270) 898-4466
E-mail: handicapable@apex.net
Web site: www.handicapable.net
Supplies: This service supplies the developmentally delayed and physically challenged youth and adults in Kentucky and surrounding states the opportunity to experience the thrills and challenges of boating, fishing and other forms of outdoor recreation.

Fishing Accessories: Electric Fishing Reels, One-Handed Fishing Vests, Fishing Pole Holders, Rods, Reels, Knives, Recreation Belts, Harnesses

Access to Recreation
8 Sandra Court
Newbury Park, CA 91320
Phone: (800) 634-4351
E-mail: dkrebs@gte.net
Web site: www.accesstr.com
Supplies: Royal Bee Electric Reels, Van's EZ Cast, One-Handed Fishing Vests

Shelton Products
5279 Salisbury Drive
Newark Ca. 94560
Phone: (510) 797 6596
E-mail: sheltonpro@aol.com
Web site: www.sheltonproducts.com
Supplies: Strikefighter Adaptive Reels

Blackberry Technology
3813 Coventryville Rd.
Pottstown, PA 19465
Phone: (800) 431-4823
Fax: (610) 469-9268
E-mail: BlkBerry@Bellatlantic.net
Web site: www.blackberrytech.com
Supplies: Integrated device designed to securely hold a fishing pole

Mann's Bait Company
111 State Docks Road
Eufaula, AL 36027
Phone: (334) 687-5716
E-mail: mannsbait@us.inter.net
Web site: www.mannsbait.com
Supplies: Belt-mounted rod holders

Flying

Freedom's Wings International
1832 Lake Avenue
Scotch Plains, NJ 07076
Phone/Fax: (908) 232-6354
E-mail: raydt@earthlink.net
Web site: www.freedomswings.org

International Wheelchair Aviators
1117 Rising Hill Way
Escondido, CA 92029
E-mail: IWAviators@aol.com
Web site: www.wheelchairaviators.org

Football

Universal Wheelchair Football Association
UC Raymond Walters College
Disability Services Office
9555 Plainfield Road
Cincinnati, OH 45236-1096
Phone: (513) 792-8625
Fax: (513) 792-8625
E-mail: johnkraimer@uc.edu

Golf

Association of Disabled American Golfers
P.O. Box 280649
Lakewood, CO 80228-0649
Phone: (303) 738-1675
Web site: www.adag.org

National Amputee Golf Association
11 Walnut Hill Rd.
Amhest, NH 03031
Phone: (800) 633-6242; (603) 672-6444
E-mail: b1naga@aol.com
Web site: www.nagagolf.org

U.S. Blind Golf Association
3094 Shamrock St. N.
Tallahassee, FL 32308-2735
Phone/Fax: (850) 893-4511
E-mail: usbga@blindgolf.com
Web site: www.blindgolf.com

Golfing Accessories: Clever Clubs or "Shorty Clubs" and Grasping Cuffs

Access to Recreation
8 Sandra Court
Newbury Park, CA 91320
Phone: (800) 634-4351
E-mail: dkrebs@gte.net
Web site: www.accesstr.com
Supplies: Clever Clubs (or shorty clubs) and Grasping Cuffs

Handcycling

Crank Chair Racing Association
3294 Lake Redding Drive
Redding, CA 96003-3311
Phone: (530) 244-3577

United States Handcycling Federation
Phone: (207) 443-3063
E-mail: info@ushf.org
Web site: www.ushf.org

Handcycling Accessories: See Chapter on Bikes

Hockey and Sled or Sledge Hockey

The U.S. Electric Wheelchair Hockey Association
7216 39th Avenue, North
Minneapolis, MN 55427
Phone: (763) 535-4736
E-mail: hockey@usewha.org
Web site: www.powerhockey.org

Canadian Electric Wheelchair Hockey Association
E-mail: info@wheelchairhockey.com
Web site: www.wheelchairhockey.com

U.S. Sled Hockey Association*
C/o Rich DeGlopper
21 Summerwood Ct.
Buffalo NY 14223
Phone: (716) 876-7390
E-mail: info@sledhockey.org
Web site: www.sledhockey.org
*"Sledge Hockey" is also called "Sled Hockey."

Hockey (Sledge) Accessories: Sleds and Sticks

Jentsch and Company Inc.
290 South Park Ave.
Buffalo NY 14204
Phone (716) 852-4111
Fax: (716) 852-4270
Supplies: Sleds

PennSled
Olympic Wheelchair Sales & Service
25 Rothsay Ave.
Kitchener, Ontario, CANADA
Phone: (519) 741-0795
Fax: (519) 741-9771
E-mail: jpenner@pennsled.com
Web site: www.pennsled.com
Supplies: Sleds

Gary Ludwig
3726 NY Rte.78
Strykersville NY 14145
Phone (716) 457-3082
E-mail: gludwig@bluemoon.net
Supplies: Sticks

Horseback Riding Therapy in the U.S. and Canada
New York Therapeutic Riding Center
336 E. 71st St., 3-D
New York, NY 10021
Phone/Fax: (212) 535-3917

North American Riding for the Handicapped Association, Inc.
P.O. Box 33150
Denver, CO 80233 USA
Phone: (800) 369-RIDE (7433); (303)-452-1212
Fax: (303) 252-4610
E-mail: www.narha@narha.org

Ice Skating
**Skating Association for the Blind and Handicapped
(SABAH) National, Inc.**
1200 East & West Road
West Seneca, NY 14224
Phone: (716) 675-SABA (7222)
Fax: (716) 675-7223
E-mail: sabah@sabahinc.org
Web site: www.sabahinc.org.

Ice Skating Accessories: Sleds, Skates, Walkers and Harnesses

Olympic Wheelchair Sales & Service
25 Rothsay Ave.
Kitchener, Ontario, CANADA
Phone: (519) 741-0795
Fax: (519) 741-9771
E-mail: jpenner@pennsled.com
Web site: www.pennsled.com
Supplies: Various Sleds

Skating Association for the Blind and Handicapped (SABAH) National, Inc.
1200 East & West Road
West Seneca, NY 14224
Phone: (716) 675-SABA (7222)
Fax: (716) 675-7223
E-mail: sabah@sabahinc.org
Web site: www.sabahinc.org
Supplies: Skates, Walkers and Harnesses

Quad Rugby

United States Quad Rugby Association
3340 E. Morrison, Apt. 380
Portland, OR 97214
Phone: (503) 238-1324
Web site: www.quadrugby.com

Quad Rugby Accessories: Sport Wheelchairs

Allegro Medical
Phone: (800) 861-3211
E-mail: Sales@AllegroMedical.com
Web site: www.allegromedical.com
Supplies: Sport Wheelchairs

Rowing

US Rowing Association
201 S. Capitol Ave., Suite 400
Indianapolis, IN 46225
Phone: (317) 237-5656
Fax: (317) 237-5646
E-mail: members@usrowing.org
Web site: www.usrowing.org

Sailing

Disabled Sailing Association of Alberta
Suite 401, 320 - 23 Ave SW
Calgary, Alberta, CanadaT2S 0J2
Phone: (403) 238-0689
Fax: (403) 249-5464
E-mail: The Commodore
Web site: www.cadvision.com

Sailing Alternatives, Inc.
7262 South Leewynn Drive
Sarasota, Florida 34240
Phone: (941) 377-4986
E-mail: info@sailingalternatives.org
Web site: www.sailingalternatives.org

SeaLegs
P.O. Box 2011
New York, NY 10159-2011
Phone: (212) 645-SAIL
E-mail: AJC2AJC3@Hamptons.com
Web site: www.gorp.com/nonprof/sealegs/classes.htm

United States Sailing Association,
P.O. Box 1260
15 Maritime Drive
Portsmouth, RI 02871-0907
Phone: (401) 683-0800
Web site: www.ussailing.org

Wheelchair Sports Associations
Sports 'N Spokes Magazine
PVA Publications
2111 E. Highland, Suite 180
Phoenix, AZ 85016
Phone: (888) 888-2201; (602) 224-0500, Ext. 19
Fax: (602) 224-0507
EMail: suzi@pnnews.com

SCUBA Diving
Handicapped SCUBA Association
1104 El Prado
San Clemente, CA 92672-4637
Phone: (949) 498-4540; (949) 498-6128
E-mail: hsa@hsascuba.com
Web site: www.hsascuba.com

Tackle Shack – SCUBA for the Disabled
St. Petersburg, FL
E-mail: Tgallag101@aol.com

Shooting and Archery
Bowhunting.Net
P.O. Box 30
Jonesboro, TX 76538
Phone/Fax: (254) 463-4215
E-mail: webmaster@bowhunting.net
Web site: www.clubs.bowhunting.net

National Wheelchair Shooting Federation
102 Park Avenue
Rockledge, PA 19046
Phone: (215) 379-2359
Fax: (215) 663-0102

NRA Disabled Shooting Services
National Rifle Association of America
11250 Waples Mill Road
Fairfax, VA 22030
Phone: (703) 267-1495
Fax: (703) 267-3941
Web site: www.nra.org

Shooting and Archery Accessories: Shooting Releases, Splints, Braces, Stands, Mouth Releases, Shooting Rests
Tru-Fire Corporation
N7355 State Street
North Fond du Lac, WI 54935-1572
Phone:(920) 923-6866
Fax: (920) 923-4051
E-mail: info@trufire.com
Web site: www.trufire.com
Supplies: Shooting Releases

Sammons Preston, An Ability One Company
General Catalog, Rehab Supplies
P.O. Box 5071
Bolingbrook, IL 60440-5071
Phone: (800) 323-5547; (800) 325-1745 (TDD)
Fax: (800) 547-4333
E-mail: sp@sammonspreston.com
Web site: www.sammonspreston.com
Supplies: Splints, Braces, Cuff.

Access to Recreation, Inc.
8 Sandra Court
Newbury Park, CA 91320
Phone: (800) 634-4351
E-mail: dkrebs@gte.net
Web site: www.accesstr.com
Supplies: Splints, Braces, Cuff.

Courage Center, REHAB Technology Dept.
3915 Golden Valley Rd.
Golden Valley, MN 55422
Phone: (800) 848-4912; (763) 588-0811
Fax: (763) 520-0577
Web site: www.courage.org
Supplies: Bow Stand, Mouth Release

R.W. (Bob) Bowen SR-77 Enterprises
363 Maple St.Chadron NE 69337
Phone: (308) 432-2894
E-mail: bob@sr77.com
Web site: www.SR77.com
Supplies: Shooting Rests

Softball
National Wheelchair Softball Association
1616 Todd Ct.
Hastings, MN 55033
Phone: (651) 437-1792
Fax: (651) 437-3889
Web site: www.wheelchairsoftball.com

Swimming

**American National Red Cross Program
of Swimming for the Handicapped**
17th and D Streets, N.W.,
Washington, DC 20006
*Contact your local American Red Cross for information

Aqua Sports Association for the Physically Challenged
9052-A Birch St.
Spring Valley, CA 91977
Phone: (619) 589-0537
Fax: (619) 589-7013

Swimming Accessories: Head Floats, Water Weights, Belt Supports, Security Belts and other Flotation Devices

Sammons Preston, An Ability One Company
General Catalog, Rehab Supplies
P.O. Box 5071
Bolingbrook, IL 60440-5071
Phone: (800) 323-5547
(800) 325-1745 (TDD)
Fax: (800) 547-4333
E-mail: sp@sammonspreston.com
Web site: www.sammonspreston.com
Supplies: Various flotation devices

Table Tennis

American Wheelchair Table Tennis Association
23 Parker Street
Port Chester, NY 10573
Phone/Fax: (914) 937-3932

Canadian Table Tennis Association
CTTC Building
2800-1125 Colonel By Drive
Ottawa, Ontario K1S 5R1 CANADA
Phone: (613) 733-6272
Fax: (613) 733-7279
E-mail: pierred@ctta.ca
Web site: www.ctta.ca

International Table Tennis Committee for the Disabled
Web site: www.tabletennis.org/ittc

Table Tennis Accessories: Grasping Cuffs (to enable player to hold onto paddle)

Access to Recreation
8 Sandra Court
Newbury Park, CA 91320
Phone: (800) 634-4351
E-mail: dkrebs@gte.net
Web site: www.accesstr.com
Supplies: Grasping Cuffs and other sports accessories

Sammons Preston, An Ability One Company
General Catalog, Rehab Supplies
P.O. Box 5071
Bolingbrook, IL 60440-5071
Phone: (800) 323-5547; (800) 325-1745 (TDD)
Fax: (800) 547-4333
E-mail: sp@sammonspreston.com
Web site: www.sammonspreston.com
Supplies: Table Tennis Cuffs

Tennis

International Wheelchair Tennis Federation
Bank Lane, Roehampton
London SW15 5XZ, England
Phone: (011) 44-181-878-6464
Fax: (011) 44-181-392-4741
Web site: www.itftennis.com

United States Tennis Association
70 West Red Oak Lane
White Plains, NY 10604
Phone: 1-888-484-8782
(914) 696-7000
Fax: (914) 696-7029
Web site: www.usta.com

Tennis Accessories: Grasping Cuffs, Orthotic Racquet Holder, Fist Grip Cuffs

Access to Recreation
8 Sandra Court
Newbury Park, CA 91320
Phone: (800) 634-4351
E-mail: dkrebs@gte.net
Web site: www.accesstr.com
Supplies: Grasping Cuffs and other sports accessories

Sammons Preston, An Ability One Company
General Catalog, Rehab Supplies
P.O. Box 5071
Bolingbrook, IL 60440-5071
Phone: (800) 323-5547; (800) 325-1745 (TDD)
Fax: (800) 547-4333
E-mail: sp@sammonspreston.com
Web site: www.sammonspreston.com
Supplies: Grasping Cuffs

Allegro Medical
Phone: (800) 861-3211
E-mail: Sales@AllegroMedical.com
Web site: www.allegromedical.com
Supplies: Sport Wheelchairs

Water Skiing

U.S.A. Waterski
1251 Holycow Road
Polk City, FL 33868
Phone: (800) 533-2972
E-mail/Web site: usa.waterski.org

Water Skiing Accessories: Manta-Ray-Water Skiing Alternative, Kan Ski and Various Flotation Devices

Access to Recreation
8 Sandra Court
Newbury Park, CA 91320
Phone: (800) 634-4351
E-mail: dkrebs@gte.net
Web site: www.accesstr.com
Supplies: Manta-Ray-Water Skiing Alternative, Kan Ski, and various flotation devices

Spokes N Motion
2225 South Platte Drive
Denver, CO 80223
Phone: (303) 922-0605
Fax: (303) 922-2943
E-mail: info@spokesnmotion.com
Web site: www.spokesnmotion.com
Supplies: Sit Skis

Access to Recreation
8 Sandra Court
Newbury Park, CA 91320
Phone: (800) 634-4351
E-mail: dkrebs@gte.net
Web site: www.accesstr.com
Supplies: Sit Skis

Weightlifting
United States Wheelchair Weightlifting Federation
39 Michael Place
Levittown, PA 19057
Phone: (215) 945-1964
Fax: (215) 946-2574

General Exercise Accessories: Rickshaw Rehabilitation Exerciser, Weight Belts, Fist Grip Cuff, Rowcycle, Handbikes, Aerobicisers, Pro II, Active Trainer, Access Trainer, Basic PT, Upper PT, Ability Flex, and more
Access to Recreation, Inc.
8 Sandra Court
Newbury Park, CA 91320
Phone: (800) 634-4351
E-mail: dkrebs@gte.net
Web site: www.accesstr.com
Supplies: Rickshaw Rehabilitation Exerciser, Therapeutic Weight Belts

Solopro
Phone: (352-367-2541
E-mail: solopro@sprynet.com
Web site: solopro.com
Supplies: Handbikes, Handbike Tables, Access Aerobicisers

No Boundaries
12882 Valley View Street, #5
Garden Grove, CA 92845
Phone: (800) 926-8637; (714) 891-5899
Fax: (714) 891-0658
Web site: www.powertrainer.com
Supplies: The A.P.T. (Active/passive trainer), Pro II, Ability Flex, Active Trainer,
Basic PT, Upper PT

General Sports and Recreation Organizations

AIM for the Handicapped
(Adventures in Movement for the Handicapped)
945 Danbury Road
Dayton, OH 45420
Phone: (800) 332-8210; (937) 294-4611
Fax: (937) 294-3783
E-mail: aimkids@siscom.net

American Alliance for Health, Physical Education,
Recreation, and Dance (AAHPERD)
1900 Association Drive
Reston, VA 20191-1599
Phone: (800) 213-7193; (703) 476-3400
Fax: (703) 476-9527
E-mail: aalr@aahperd.org
Web site: www.aahperd.org/aalr.html

American Amputee Foundation, Inc.
P.O. Box 250218
Little Rock, AR 72225
Phone (501) 666-2523
Fax: (501) 666-8367

American Athletic Association of the Deaf
3916 Lantern Drive
Silver Spring, MD 20902

American Cancer Society
Home Office
1599 Clifton Rd. NE
Atlanta, GA 30329-4251
Phone: (800) 227-2345
Web site: www.cancer.org

American Printing House for the Blind
1839 Frankfort Avenue
Louisville, KY 40206
Phone: (800) 572-0844; (502) 895-2405
Fax: (502) 899-2274
E-mail: info@aph.org
Web site: www.aph.org

Amputee Sports Organization
11705 Mercy Boulevard
Savannah, GA 31406

Association of Handicapped Artists
5150 Broadway
Depew, NY 14043

Beneficial Designs, Inc.
1617 Water St., Ste 13
Mindon, NV 89423
Phone: (775) 783-8822
Fax: (831) 423-8450
E-mail: mail@beneficialdesigns.com
*Designs Adaptive sporting equipment

Blind Outdoor Leisure Development
533 E. Main Street
Aspen, CO 81611

Canadian Amputee Sports Association
217 Holmes Avenue
Willowdale, ON M2N 4M9
Phone: (416) 222-8625
Fax: (416) 229-6547
E-mail: ampsport@interlog.com
Web site: www.interlog.com/~ampsport/can_amputee.html

Canadian Wheelchair Sports Association
333 River Road
Ottawa, Ontario K1L 8H9
CANADA

Courage Center
3915 Golden Valley Rd.
Golden Valley, MN 55422
Phone: (763) 588-0811
Fax: (763) 520-0577
E-mail: sports@courage.com
Web site: www.courage.org

Department of the Interior
Accessibility Management Program
P.O. Box 37127
Washington, DC 20013
Phone: (202) 208-3100
Fax: (202) 343-3674
E-mail: david_park@nps.gov

Department of Recreation
CB#3185, Evergreen House
730 Airport Rd. UNC
Chapel Hill, NC 27599-3185
Phone: (919) 962-0534
Fax: (919) 962-1223
E-mail: kluken@email.unc.edu

Disabled Sports USA (DSUSA)
451 Hungerford Dr., Suite 100
Rockville, MD 20850
Phone: (301) 217-0960
TDD: (301) 217-0963
Fax: (301) 217-0968
E-mail: information@dsusa.org
Web site: www.dsusa.org

Dwarf Athletic Club of America
418 Willow Way
Lewisville, TX 75067
Phone: (972) 317-8299

Houston Challengers *Wheelchair Sports
1475 West Gray, Suite 166
Houston, TX 77018-4926
Phone: (713) 521-3737

International Committee of the Silent Sports
Callaudet College
Florida Avenue and Seventh Streets, N.E.
Washington, DC 20002

National Ability Center (NAC)
P.O. Box 682799
Park City, UT 84068-2799
Phone/TDD: (435) 649-3991
Fax: (435) 649-3992
E-mail: nac@xmission.com
Web site: www.nationalabilitycenter.org

National Center on Accessibility
University of Indiana
2805 E. 10th St., Ste. 190
Bloomington, IN 47408
Phone: (812) 856-4422
TDD: (812) 856-4421
Fax: (812) 856-4480
E-mail: nca@indiana.edu
Web site: www.ncaonline.org

National Center on Physical Activity and Disability
University of Illinois at Chicago
Dept. of Disability and Human Development
College of Applied And Health Sciences
1640 West Roosevelt Rd.
Chicago, IL 60698
Phone/TDD: (800) 900-8086
Fax: (312) 355-4058
E-mail: ncpad@uic.edu
Web site: www.ncpad.org

National Ocean Access Project
Hazel E. Stark Center
Chester, CT 06412

National Sports Center for the Disabled (NSCD)
P.O. Box 1290
Winter Park, CO 80482
Phone: (970) 726-1540 or (303) 316-1540
Fax: (970) 726-4112
Denver Office: 633 17th St. Ste. 24
Denver, CO 80202
Phone: (303) 293-5711, Fax: (303) 293.5446
E-mail: info@nscd.org
Web site: www.nscd.org

Paralyzed Veterans of America
801 18th St. NW
Washington, DC 20006
Phone: (800) 424-8200
Fax: (202) 955-8358 (fax)
E-mail: bruces@pva.org
Web site: www.pva.org

Special Olympics, International
1325 G. Street NW, Suite 500
Washington, DC 20005
Phone: (202) 628-3630
Fax: (202) 824-0200
E-mail: soimail@aol.com
Web site: www.specialolympics.org

U.S. Amputee Athletic Association
P.O. Box 210709
Nashville, TN 37221

U.S. Association for Blind Athletes
33 N. Institute, Brown Hall,
Colorado Springs, CO 80903
Phone: (719) 630-0422
Fax: (719) 630-0616
E-mail: dtumai@USABA.org
Web site: www.usaba.org

U.S. Cerebral Palsy Athletic Association (USCPAA)
25 W. Independence Way
Kingston, RI 02881
Phone: (401) 874-7465
Fax: (401) 874-7468
E-mail: uscpaa@mail.bbsnet.com
Web site: www.uscpaa.org

U.S. Deaf Sports Federation
3607 Washington Blvd., Suite 4
Ogden, UT 84403-1737
Phone: (888) 735-5906 (voice relay)
TDD: (801) 393-7916
Fax: (801) 393-2263
E-mail: homeoffice@usadsf.org

U.S. Les Autres Sports Association
1475 W. Gray, Ste. 166
Houston, TX 77019
(713) 521-3737

Wheelchair Sports, USA
3595 E. Fountain Blvd., Suite L-1
Colorado Springs, CO 80910
Phone: (719) 574-1150

Hyperbaric Oxygen Therapy (HBOT)

The following three reports have been reproduced with permission from the United Cerebral Palsy Research & Education Foundation. These well-written review articles discuss the clinical use and ongoing research, including the yet unanswered research questions concerning Hyperbaric Oxygen Therapy (HBOT) in the treatment of cerebral palsy and other brain injuries.

For more information and recent research updates contact the UCP National (also known as United Cerebral Palsy), 1660 L Street, NW, Suite 700, Washington, DC 20036. Phone: 800-872-5827/202-776-0406 TTY: 202-973-7197 Fax: 202-776-0414, e-mail: webmaster@ucp.org, Web site: http://www.ucpa.org/ucp_general.cfm/1/4 , go to Research Foundation & Fact Sheets, Research Fact Sheets, then Sections, then Diagnosing and/or Treatment.

Hyperbaric Oxygen Therapy for the Treatment of Cerebral Palsy, 9/1999

Status Report on Unsubstantiated Interventions, September 1999

FOREWORD

Cerebral palsy and other neurodevelopmental disorders are characterized by the presence of functional impairments and disabilities that can interfere with activities of daily living. Conventional therapies and interventions often do improve functional status but may not provide the degree of functional improvement and independence that persons with a disability, their parents or caregivers desire. As a result, a number of unsubstantiated approaches to improve function have been proposed in the past and new but unsubstantiated approaches are regularly being offered. Some are based upon new applications of methods used for other purposes; others are a reformulation and combination of accepted practices; and others are founded on ideas and practices that are at variance with currently accepted concepts of human biology and clinical care. There is often an initial burst of enthusiasm about results by those participating in unconventional interventions; however, the enthusiasm generally disappears as the results are found to be less than expected, only transitory, or not beneficial enough to justify the additional investment in time or funds.

Unsubstantiated interventions are rarely supported by research studies that meet accepted standards. The reports are often anecdotal; that is, the observation of participants about their own or someone else's experience. On occasion, a report of an organized series of experiences is available (a "case series"). However, none of these reports provides the type of evidence required to make an accurate judgment about the intervention's safety, its adequacy or its relative benefit. Also, there is generally no organized body of reliable evidence to demonstrate when the intervention fails to work. Failure is rarely reported in anecdotal reports of unsubstantiated treatments. As important as anecdotal reports can be to draw attention to an unsubstantiated intervention, only carefully designed clinical trials can provide the evidence necessary to properly assess its role and the appropriateness of its incorporation as part of "mainstream" treatment.

Unsubstantiated approaches that propose to diminish disability and improve function, but which have not been evaluated in carefully designed clinical trials are regularly being offered to the public. In order to be of assistance, we offer these comments on hyperbaric oxygenation in the treatment of cerebral palsy so that the public can come to decisions based on what is known and not known at this time.

HYPERBARIC OXYGEN FOR CEREBRAL PALSY: A STATUS REPORT

Hyperbaria is the term used to describe a procedure in which a person is placed in an enclosed chamber in which the atmospheric pressure of air is gradually increased, maintained, and then gradually decreased. It is used for the treatment of decompression illness ("the bends"), a condition brought on by too rapid decompression when coming to the surface rapidly after a deep dive or when people working under increased atmospheric pressure return to normal atmospheric pressure too rapidly (e.g. escaping from undersea vessels; building tunnels under rivers).

Hyperbaric oxygenation is the term used to describe a procedure in which an increased amount of oxygen is added to the air breathed under hyperbaric conditions, sometimes 100% oxygen. Under increased pressure, oxygen is made more available to red blood cells (the usual transporters of oxygen in the blood); in addition, oxygen is also dissolved in the fluid (plasma) of the blood. Thus, additional oxygen becomes available to the body's tissues as the oxygen-enriched blood circulates.

Hyperbaric oxygenation is medically accepted for use in a number of conditions including the treatment of carbon monoxide poisoning, gangrene, skin ulceration and sometimes to support the growth of skin grafts used in the treatment of burns. It is not a harmless procedure in that too much oxygen can be very harmful to tissues and can cause important blood vessels in the brain and heart to constrict; also oxygen under pressure may cause a pneumothorax (collapsed lung). The delivery of hyperbaric oxygen must be done by experts under very carefully controlled conditions.

During the past few years, a few clinicians have explored the use of hyperbaric oxygenation in a variety of conditions such as stroke, head injury, spinal cord injury, and multiple sclerosis. At this time, the published scientific literature does not support the use of this technique in any of these conditions. A major problem has been the lack of well-designed clinical trials utilizing a scientifically acceptable protocol to evaluate the usefulness of the procedure for these conditions. Reports of success are anecdotal and are very difficult to evaluate for reliability or validity. On the other hand, neither has it been demonstrated that the procedure fails to work. Thus, there is no acceptable evidence available at this time to support either conclusion: it works; it doesn't work.

This is also true at this time in regard to the use of hyperbaric oxygenation in the treatment of developmental brain damage such as cerebral palsy or in the treatment of the impairments (e.g. spasticity) or disabilities (e.g. decreased mobility) associated with it. There is no scientifically acceptable evidence available at this time that demonstrates its clinical usefulness; neither is there any scientifically acceptable evidence available at this time demonstrating its lack of usefulness. Individual stories ("anecdotes") tell very little; they are interesting, provocative, but not scientifically informative.

Comment

There is no biological basis for assuming that increased oxygen availability will have any effect on established lesions due to a developmental brain disorder in the brain of a person with disabilities.

However, it is believed by some of the proponents of hyperbaric oxygenation that there are areas adjacent to the brain lesion which they consider to be non-functional but alive; they also believe these areas can be made functional by hyperbaric oxygenation and that this will result in improved performance. It is also believed by some proponents that unaffected or undamaged areas of the brain will be stimulated by increased oxygen availability and will take over the function of damaged areas of the brain. These are hypotheses that need to be tested. As of now, they are based on conjecture and on inferences drawn from poorly designed or unrelated studies.

The clinical usefulness of hyperbaric oxygen therapy in the treatment of the disabilities associated with cerebral palsy is presently based only on individual anecdotes. Its usefulness has not been put to the test using research methods essential for its evaluation. A few clinical case series have been reported; a few pilot studies utilizing organized protocols of evaluation are said to have been done, but the methodologies and their results have not been published in the peer reviewed scientific literature.

Although not yet demonstrated, it is conceivable that hyperbaric oxygenation may be of help to selected persons with certain kinds of disabilities. If it is helpful, it is not known whether beneficial effects are short-lived or permanent. It is also conceivable that any positive results at best are marginal and/or temporary. Finally, it is equally conceivable that hyperbaric oxygenation has no beneficial effects.

We urge clinicians who support the use of hyperbaric oxygenation in the treatment of disabilities associated with cerebral palsy to develop and launch well-designed clinical trials to evaluate its usefulness and to publish their results so the medical community can review them and the public can be informed. The initiative for these studies is theirs; the responsibility is theirs to demonstrate that what they believe is true.

For the time being, we urge persons interested in the use of hyperbaric oxygenation in cerebral palsy to be cautious about the interpretation of anecdotes about its usefulness and we encourage families to seek advice from a number of professionals and families who have had their children participate. Also, we urge families to make certain that the physicians providing the therapy are expert in BOTH hyperbaric medicine and in developmental brain injury.

NOTE:

At a scientific meeting in Toronto, Canada, on September 23, 2000, a research group from McGill University presented its results of a controlled clinical trial of hyperbaric oxygen therapy in the treatment of disabilities associated with cerebral palsy. Over 100 children were evaluated, half receiving hyperbaric oxygen and the other half receiving regular air under the same conditions. The results showed no difference between the two groups.

UCP Research & Educational Foundation, September 1999

Hyperbaric Oxygen Therapy (HBO) for Children with Cerebral Palsy: Report of a Clinical Trial, 2/2001

BACKGROUND

100% oxygen given under increased pressure in a hyperbaric chamber (HBO) will increase the amount of oxygen in the blood; as a result, additional oxygen can be delivered to cells and tissues of the body. HBO has been found useful in the treatment of several disorders such as decompression illness, carbon monoxide poisoning and in assisting skin grafting in the treatment of burns. It also has been tried in a number of chronic neurological disorders, generally with little success. The effects of HBO therapy in acute brain injury (e.g. head trauma) is being evaluated. It has been speculated by some that increased oxygen given to children with cerebral palsy will restore some function. In recent years, a number of reports of success have been circulated by advocates of the method, including parents of children. However, these reports are extremely difficult to evaluate for a host of reasons. Thus, a carefully designed and scientifically acceptable clinical trial was sorely needed to tell us about the usefulness of HBO in the treatment of children with disabilities due to cerebral palsy.

The American Academy of Cerebral Palsy and Developmental Medicine, Web site: http://www.aacpdm.org, is a professional society whose membership includes physicians and clinical therapists engaged in research and in the care of persons with disabilities due to disorders of the developing brain. At its annual meeting, important new findings are presented and discussed. At its September 2000 meeting, two sessions were held on hyperbaric oxygen therapy (HBO) for children with disabilities due to cerebral palsy; one session was the presentation and discussion of a clinical research trial of HBO and the other was a public forum addressing the public experience with HBO and the implications for clinical care of the results of the trial.

SUMMARY OF THE PRESENTATION OF THE CLINICAL RESEARCH TRIAL[1]

Methodology

The results of a clinical trial were presented which assessed the "effects of hyperbaric oxygen therapy in children with cerebral palsy".

The trial was organized and conducted as multi-centered (several participating institutions using the same protocol), randomized (children were assigned by "chance" to one of two treatment groups), and double-blinded (neither the children nor the evaluating therapists were aware of the treatment given). This is the methodology recognized internationally as the "gold standard" for the scientific evaluation of a clinical intervention. Five treatment centers were involved, each skilled in the care of children with cerebral palsy and in the use of hyperbaria. The trial included 111 children with spastic cerebral palsy (spastic diplegia, spastic quadriplegia or spastic double hemiplegia). The children were of ages 3-12 and had a cognitive age of greater than 24 months. They were randomized into two treatment groups: one group—the HBO treatment group—received 100% oxygen at 1.75 atmospheric pressure in a hyperbaric chamber; the other group—the non-HBO treatment group—- received regular air at 1.3 atmospheric pressure in a hyperbaric chamber (1.3 atmospheric pressure is considered physiologically comparable to non-hyperbaric air) and similar to oxygen administered by a nasal tube. Treatments were given to each group for 5 days a week for 8 weeks. The children in both groups were evaluated using standardized scales for evaluation of function, spasticity, speech and cognition prior to therapy, again after 20 treatments, again after 40 treatments and finally 3 months after treatment ended.

Results

Of the 111 children who entered the trial, 107 completed the trial (54 HBO and 53 non-HBO). Before the clinical interventions (either HBO or non-HBO), both groups were comparable on the evaluations listed above.

The results showed significant improvement in SOME children in BOTH groups. From the data, the following was felt to be true:

- both HBO and non HBO were equally effective;
- the use of HBO did not do anything in itself; but participation in the trial had a beneficial effect on some children;
- the children showed a "learning effect" in responding to the same evaluations repeatedly;
- both groups also showed improvements due to normal development.

Conclusions

Participation in the study alone had a beneficial effect; however, HBO as such had no effect.

COMMENT

First, it is important to understand that the above summary is that of the UCP Research and Educational Foundation and was not written by the study's authors. We believe it to be an accurate description of their presentations. Also, the Foundation rarely distributes the results of a study until they have been published in a scientific journal. We have been informed that the manuscript reporting on the study has been accepted for publication, but it will be some time before publication actually occurs. Because of public interest in the usefulness of HBO in the treatment of disabilities due to cerebral palsy, the Foundation felt it appropriate to distribute the above summary at this time.

From research technical and operational viewpoints, this clinical trial is excellent. From the clinical care viewpoint, the study's results raise serious doubt about the usefulness of hyperbaric oxygen in the treatment of the disabilities associated with cerebral palsy. Critics of the study and of the interpretation of its results feel that (1) the level of HBO provided was too high; (2) it was not administered over a long enough period; (3) although the study population was randomized, the two groups were not similar enough; and (4) the conclusions drawn were inappropriate.

As other trials have demonstrated, it certainly indicates that participation in a focused endeavor (i.e. a clinical trial) in itself can have beneficial effects on function for a child with disabilities due to cerebral palsy. Thus, a scientifically acceptable trial must be able to sort out beneficial effects due to the intervention being tested from beneficial effects due to participation (the latter often a result of increased motivation and increased and prolonged structured attention).

Is this the final word on the usefulness of HBO? Probably not. It could be useful to repeat this study in another location to learn if the results are the same (validation). Also, a careful analysis of the data from this study might reveal the characteristics of a sub-population of children who may appear to have been assisted by HBO when compared to a similar group who did not receive HBO. The numbers of children in that sub-population may have been too small to demonstrate a useful effect. If such a sub-population can be identified, a randomized, double blind trial of that group would be warranted. Finally, if different levels and duration of HBO are thought by some to be better, they can be tested—but tested against a non-HBO population.

This was an excellent and much needed study. It told us a great deal about several things—including that good scientific studies can be done for evaluating the usefulness of interventions on the function of children with disabilities due to cerebral palsy. Society requires such studies; parents need them; the children deserve them.

Note: On February 24, 2001, an internationally prestigious medical research journal published the details of the HBO Trial discussed above: The Lancet 2001, Vol. 357, pgs 586-586. As published, the authors state: "Interpretation (of results) in this study, hyperbaric oxygen did not improve the condition of children with cerebral palsy compared with slightly pressurized air. The improvement seen in both groups for all dimensions tested deserves further consideration".

1. Presented by Jean-Paul Collet MD,MSc,PhD and colleagues; summarized in the "AACPDM NEWS" (Dec 2000); Vol 50 #2; pg 7

UCP Research & Educational Foundation, February 2001

Hyperbaric Oxygen Therapy In the Treatment of Brain Injury: Report of a Meeting, 8/2001

On July 25-28, 2001, a meeting was held in which clinicians, clinical investigators and family members reviewed the present status of information about the use of hyperbaric oxygen therapy (HBOT) in the treatment of brain injury.[1] Nearly all participants in the meeting were advocates of the use of HBOT; there were no presentations by conferees who were either opposed to the use of the therapy for this purpose or whose position was as yet undecided. One of the major topics of discussion was the recent report of the "Montreal trial" that demonstrated significant functional improvement in many of the cerebral palsy children participating in the randomized, double-blinded HBOT trial, but with no differences in functional outcomes in children treated either with 1.35 ATA of air or 1.75 ATA of 100% oxygen.

The conferees participated in two broad areas of discussion: (1) reports of clinical experiences that appeared to preserve life and restore impaired function when HBOT was administered soon after brain injury (e.g. traumatic brain injury; drowning; birth hypoxia; meningitis); and (2) the clinical experience that HBOT appeared to restore function in persons (usually children) with disabilities following brain injury at sometime in the past (e.g. cerebral palsy).

At this meeting, the principle presentations were reports of clinical experience utilizing HBOT, either individual cases or case series. The reports described functional improvement in both the acute and chronic situations following brain injury. In the chronic situation (cerebral palsy), the results of the use of 100% oxygen administered at a variety of atmospheric pressures were discussed (1.75 ATA; 1.5 ATA; 1.35 ATA); all were reported to be associated with positive short term and long term results; no reports were presented that described poor results. The recognized danger of hyperbaric oxygen was discussed (i.e. seizures), as were the less well recognized behavioral manifestations of oxygen toxicity (e.g. agitation; aggressiveness). In the experience of the conferees, it appears that these complications are unusual, but when they do occur they are manageable by the termination of therapy and the use later of lower levels of hyperbaric oxygen.

One focused item of conference discussion was the Montreal trial and the "implication" that the control subjects receiving air at 1.35 ATA were receiving a "placebo" (a non-therapeutic intervention). It was stated by clinical participants at the conference that air at 1.35 ATA increased both the oxygen level of red blood cells and caused oxygen in the air to dissolve in the blood's fluid (plasma); both increased the availability of oxygen to body tissues—including the brain.

It was proposed by several conferees that the control group of the subjects in the Montreal study were also receiving an increased oxygen supply to the brain; thus explaining the similar clinical improvement in both segments of the study population. If this is true, should air administered at 1.35 ATA be used instead of HBOT? The question was asked, but not answered.

In support of the effects of HBOT on the brain, a number of brain imaging studies using SPECT before and after treatment were presented. SPECT provides images of regional cerebral blood flow; by inference, a change in blood flow implies but does not demonstrate a change in cerebral metabolism. In all of the cases presented, SPECT showed increase in cerebral blood flow in a variety of poorly perfused areas of the brain following HBOT. It was hypothesized that these areas of increased blood flow were metabolically more active than prior to HBOT.

COMMENT:

The reports presented at this meeting of improved function and cerebral circulation cannot be disregarded by labeling them as "observations by biased advocates". These observations by skilled clinicians and parents need to be explored by appropriate scientific studies that meet the standards of modern research. One study, the Montreal study, clearly indicates that room air delivered at a low level of increased atmospheric pressure (1.35 ATA) gives identical results to 100% oxygen delivered at increased pressure (1.75 ATA). At this time, there is still no scientifically acceptable evidence that HBOT is useful in the treatment of disabilities associated with Cerebral Palsy. The following questions remain to be answered:

• Is HBOT (oxygen level? pressure level?) useful in the treatment of disabilities associated with cerebral palsy?

- Is hyperbaria alone (pressure level?) useful in the treatment of disabilities associated with cerebral palsy?
- Is oxygen supplementation alone (oxygen level?) useful in the treatment of disabilities associated with cerebral palsy?

Sufficient clinical experience does exist to support the need for additional controlled studies exploring these questions in a scientifically acceptable manner (i.e. randomized, double-blind trials). Air delivered in a hyperbaric chamber at 1.0 ATA can serve as a control.

Another issue also requires study: the suggestion that there are "idling" neurons in the brain years after injury that become active after the use of HBOT. At this time, there is no evidence that this is true. However, there are methods available to test this hypothesis: PET brain imaging or metabolic magnetic imaging. These quantitative methods of measuring focal brain metabolism can be applied before & after HBOT and will answer the question.

Are the above studies do-able? They are. To be successful they must have the active participation of the children to be studied, their care-givers, clinicians, and scientists. They also require the organizational arrangements and financial resources that these studies demand in order to be successful. The UCP Research and Educational Foundation is attempting to see if the necessary personnel, the organizational and the financial requirements can be mobilized to initiate these needed studies to evaluate the usefulness of HBOT in treating children with dis-abilities due to cerebral palsy.

1International Symposium on Hyperbaric Oxygen in Cerebral Palsy and the Brain/Injured Child. Boca Raton, Florida; July 25-28, 2001. Richard A. Neubauer, MD, Chairman

Service Dogs

"Children and dogs are as necessary to the welfare of
the country as Wall Street and the railroads."

President Harry S. Truman

Dogs are used as service animals, not only for children and adults
with visual impairments (guide dogs) and hearing impairments
(hearing dogs), but now to assist those that are physically disabled
(assistance dogs) or have seizures (seizure-response dogs). As recently
reviewed by medical researchers Dr. Allen and Dr. Blascovich, service
dogs have been specifically trained to assist individuals with many different tasks, including opening and closing doors, pulling wheelchairs,
helping a person in or out of bed, bathtub or pool, retrieving objects,
carrying items in the store, and rescuing a person in case of a fire or
other emergencies (Source: Allen, K and J. Blascovich. The value of
service dogs for people with severe ambulatory disabilities: a randomized, controlled trial. *Journal of the American Medical Association*, Vol
275(13), April 3, 1996, 1001-1006).

Dr. Allen and Dr. Blascovich also discovered that service dogs help
persons with disabilities by improving their self-esteem and well being
as well as aiding public acceptance and community integration, and
increasing school attendance and/or part-time employment. Service
dogs allowed for greater independence with less assistance, paid and
unpaid, being needed to care for those persons who had service dogs.
These researchers concluded, "Trained service dogs can be highly beneficial and potentially cost-effective components of independent living
for people with physical disabilities."

Service dogs can provide comfort, independence and improved mobility at home, at school and out in the community. Children enjoy their new independence and develop a close friendship with either a formally trained service dog or a gentle, responsive family dog. By using an inexpensive dogsled-type harness, children are:

- Enjoying year-round hiking with family and with friends
- Playing with neighborhood kids in the backyard
- Playing out in the deep snow and sledding or tobogganing by being able to walk independently back up the hill with their dog at their side.

These inexpensive dog harnesses, such as the "Step in harness," range from approximately $5.00 to $9.00 for large dogs or the "Pro-Stop! No-Tug Harness" for approximately $14.00, which can be purchased from:

R.C. Steele, Inc.
1989 Transit Way
Brockport, NY 14420
Phone: (800) 287-9073 retail store, (800) 872-3773
Web site: www.rcsteele.com , click on Dogs, and either use their *Fetch* (Search) Feature for dog harnesses or type in "Step in harness"

Use of a service dog cannot exclude any individual from restaurants, public parks, or any public transportation, including walking aboard an aircraft. This is in accordance with U.S. federal law (Americans with Disabilities Act: Public Law (PL)101-336, July 26, 1990; Rehabilitation Act of 1973 and the 1992 Amendments to the Rehabilitation Act). For example in New York State, New York State Civil Rights Law (§§40-c and 47-c (McKinney Supp. 1991)) states:

(A) No person shall be denied admittance to and/or the equal use of and enjoyment of any public facility solely because said person is disabled and is accompanied by a guide, hearing or service dog.
(1) "Public facility" includes, but is not limited to, all modes of public and private transportation, all forms of public and private housing accommodations, buildings to which the public is invited, all educational facilities, all places where food is offered

for sale, all theaters, playhouses and all other places of public accommodations, convenience, resort, entertainment, or business to which the general public may be invited or permitted. Violation may result in a penalty of $100 - $500 – payable to the aggrieved party and conviction of a Class A Misdemeanor.

Another very helpful source of specific information on the rights of individuals with service dogs is Mr. Richard Vargas at the New York State Office of Advocate for Persons with Disabilities, (1-800-522-4369).

With airplane travel, service dogs weighing up to approximately 75 pounds can easily be trained to curl up under the aircraft seat in front of the child or adult. You may also request seating behind a bulkhead (the divider between first class and coach) for more leg room and convenience. For more information on service dog training, contact your local veterinarian. Your veterinarian may also provide you with a written statement regarding your dog having received adequate training as a service dog. All service dogs must be medically examined and you must have a health certificate from your veterinarian within ten days prior to flying the initial leg of your trip, according to the Federal Aviation Administration (FAA).

There are also many organizations dedicated to training dogs to assist children and adults with various disabilities to lead more independent and secure lives. Hearing dogs alert hearing-impaired persons to various sounds in the environment. Assistance or service dogs assist physically disabled individuals with common tasks that are difficult or impossible to accomplish. Mobility or multi-service dogs perform a variety of tasks for individuals with multiple disabilities or special needs. Therapy or companion dogs provide close companionship for individuals or residents of institutions.

For more information on service dogs, contact the following organizations:

Assistance Dog Institute
P.O. Box 2334
Rohnert Park, CA 94927-2334
Phone: (707) 585-0300, (707) 537-6391
Fax: (707) 537-1954
E-mail: assistdog@aol.com
Web site: www.assistancedog.org
*Assistance dogs, social therapy-facilties dogs, helpmates

Assistance Dog United Campaign
P.O. Box 2804
Rohnert Park, CA 94927-2804
Phone: (800) 284-DOGS (284-3647)
Fax: (707) 537-1952
*Offers vouchers for assistance dogs based on financial need.

Canine Assistants
3160 Francis Road
Alpharetta, Georgia 30004
Phone: (800) 771-7221; (770) 664-7178
Fax: (770) 664-7820
Web site: www.canineassistants.org
*Canine Assistants, founded in 1991, trains and provides service dogs for children and adults with physical disabilities or other special needs. Canine Assistants service dogs are useful in removing many of the challenges and barriers faced by the disabled in today's society.

Canine Companions for Independence
P.O. Box 446
Santa Rosa, CA 95402-0446
Phone: (800) 572-BARK (572-2275)
or National Headquarters at (866) CCI-DOGS (224-3647)
Fax: (707) 577-1711
E-mail: info@caninecompanions.org
Web site: www.caninecompanions.org
*Assistance dogs, hearing dogs, companion dogs and faciltity team dogs.

Canine Companions for Independence (Ohio)
4989 St. Tr. 37 E.
Delaware, OH 43015
Phone: (740) 548-4447
Fax: (740) 363-0555

Canine Companions for Independence (Chicago Satellite Office)
P.O. Box 41
Woodstock, IL 60098
Phone: (847) 816-7360
Fax: (847) 816-7361
Web site: www.cci-chicago.org

Canine Helpers for the Handicapped, Inc.
5705 Ridge Rd.
Lockport, NY 14094
Phone: (716)433-4035
Web site: http://caninehelpers.netfirms.com
*Assistance, hearing, guide and therapy dogs

Delta Society
289 Perimeter Road E.
Renton, WA 98055-1329
Phone: (800) 869-6898, (425) 226-7357
Fax: (206) 808-7601, (425) 235-1076
E-mail: info@deltasociety.org
Web site: www.deltasociety.org
*Dog assistance referrral program with a national directory, and many resources.

Fidos for Freedom
P.O. Box 5508
Laurel, MD 20726
Phone: (410) 880-4178, (301) 570-7770 (TTY)
Fax: (301) 776-7749
E-mail: fidos@erols.com
Web site: www.fidosforfreedom.org
*Assistance Dogs and hearing dogs.

Freedom Service Dogs
P.O. Box 150217
Lakewood, CO 80215
Phone: (303) 234-9512
Fax: (303) 237-3878
*Assistance dogs for the physically disabled only, with no hearing or guide dogs.

International Association of Assistance Dog Partners
38691 Filly Dr.
Sterling Heights, MI 48311
Phone: (810) 826-3938
E-mail: iaadp@ismi.net
Web site: www.ismi.net/iaadp/index/html
*Information and referral for guide, assistance and hearing dog services.

Mile High Hearing and Handi Dogs
P.O. Box 734
Littleton, CO 80134
Phone: (303) 288-7297
*Assistance dogs and hearing dogs

Paws with a Cause
4646 S. Division
Wayland, MI 49348
Phone: (800) 253-7297
Fax: (616) 877-0248
E-mail: paws@alliance.net
Web site: www.ismi.net/paws
*Assistance dogs, seizure response dogs and hearing dogs.

For Guide Dogs to assist the blind, contact the following organizations:

Guiding Eyes for the Blind
611 Granite Springs Road
Yorktown Heights, NY 10598
Phone: (800) 942-0149, (914) 245-4024
Fax: (914) 245-1609
Web site: www.guiding-eyes.org/Default.htm

Leader Dogs for the Blind
P.O. Box 5000
Rochester, MI 48308
Phone: (888) 777-5332, (248) 651-9011
E-mail: Leaderdog@leaderdog.org
Web site: www.leaderdog.com

Pilot Dogs, Inc.
625 W. Town St.
Columbus, OH 43215
Phone: (614) 221-6367

Seeing Eye, Inc.
P.O. Box 375
Morristown, NJ 07963-0375
Phone: (973) 539-0922
Fax: (973) 539-0922
E-mail: semaster@seeingeye.org
Web site: www.seeingeye.org

The Seeing Eye in Canada
105 Gordon Baker Rd.
Willowdale, ON M2H 3P8
CANADA
Web site: www.seeingeye.org and click on Canada

Southeastern Guide Dogs, Inc.
4210 77th St. East
Palmetto, FL 34221
Phone: (941) 729-5665
Fax: (941) 729-6646
Web site: www.guidedogs.org

For recreation therapy using service dogs, contact:

Ms. Michelle Saffire, Recreation Therapist
Western New York Developmental Disability Service Office
Building 9
1200 East and West Road.
West Seneca, NY 14224
Phone: (716) 674-6300, ext. 3825

Suggested reading:

**"The Healing Power of Pets: Harnessing the Amazing Power of Pets
to Make and Keep People Happy and Healing"**
Author: Marty Becker, DVM with Danelle Morton
Pets/HealthFebruary 2003
272 pages
$14.95US/$22.95CAN
ISBN: 0-7868-8691-9
Web site: www.hyperionbooks.com

Magazines

Active Living
2276 Rosedene Road
St. Ann's, Ontario L0R 1Y0, CANADA
Phone: (905) 957-6016
Fax: (905) 957-6017
E-mail: activeliv@aol.com
Web site: www.activelivingmagazine.com
*"The Health, Fitness & Recreation Magazine for People With a Disability"

The Exceptional Parent
P.O. Box 2078
Marion, OH 43306-2178
Phone: 877-372-7368
Web site: www.eparent.com
*Featuring information and support for the special needs community
including parents, families, physicians and professionals.

Family Life
P.O. Box 23840
Little Rock, AR 72221-3840.
Phone: (800) FL-TODAY (1-800-358-6329), 1-877-FL-TODAY (Español)
Web site: http://www.familylife.com
* Family Life offers tools to build strong homes, including conferences since
1976 and multiple resources like the HomeBuilders Couples Series®, FamilyLife
Marriage Conference, and a daily radio program, "FamilyLife Today," providing
practical, biblical answers to the issues couples and families face.

Focus on the Family
8605 Explorer Drive
Colorado Springs, CO 80920-1051
Phone: (719) 531-5181
Web site: www.family.org
*Mission Statement: To cooperate with the Holy Spirit in disseminating the Gospel of Jesus Christ to as many people as possible, and, specifically, to accomplish that objective by helping to preserve traditional values and the institution of the family.

in Motion
Amputee Coalition of America
900 E. Hill Ave., Ste. 285
Knoxville, TN 37915-2568
Phone: (888) AMP-KNOW (267-5669)
(865) 524-8772
E-mail: editor@amputee-coalition.org
Web site: http://www.amputee-coalition.org
*A Publication of the National Limb Loss Information Center

Mainstream Magazine
P.O. Box 370598
San Diego, CA 92137-0598
Web site: http://www.mainstream-mag.com
*An invaluable on-line resource magazine for the able-disabled, providing News & Advocacy in Disability Rights.

PACER Center, Inc.
8161 Normandale Blvd.
Minneapolis, Minnesota 55437
Phone: (800) 53PACER (537-2237; (952) 838-9000; TTY: (952) 838-0190
Toll-free in Greater Minnesota: (800) 537-2237
Fax: (952) 838-0199 E-mail: pacer@pacer.org
Web site: www.pacer.org.
*A news magazine for parents of children and young people with disabilities featuring programs, networking, and peer-support with download publications for parents facing the difficulties of raising a child with a disability.

Palaestra
Circulation Department, Challenge Publications
P.O. Box 508
Macomb, IL 61455
Fax: (309) 833-1902
Web site: www.palaestra.com
*Palaestra is a magazine for those with disabilities, their parents and professionals concerning sport, physical education and recreation.

Parenting
P.O. Box 52424
Boulder, CO 80323-2424
Web site: www.parenting.com
*From the publisher of Child, Family Circle, and McCall's, Parents Magazine
publishes regularly updated reports and advice on the usual issues for parents.

Trade Shows and Conferences

World Congress & Exposition on Disabilities
WCD
210 Route 4 East
Paramus, NJ 07652
Phone: (877) 923-3976, ext. 832
(201) 226-1446
Fax: (201) 226-1236
E-mail and Web site: www.wcdexpo.com
*This annual disability conference and trade show brings together families, therapists, physicians, direct support professionals, people with disabilities, allied healthcare professionals, educators, adapted physical education and sports therapy specialists, media sponsors, educational sponsors and supporting organizations.

The Accessibility Show (formerly AccessAbilities EXPO*)
334 Carlisle Avenue
York, PA 17404
Phone: (717) 848-2596 - Grandstand Tickets: (717) 848-2033
E-mail: info@yorkfair.org
Web site: www.yorkfair.org The Accessibility Show features products and services designed to enhance the lives of people with disabilities, their families and caregivers. Manufacturers demonstrate the latest equipment and products and service-related companies and organizations provide additional valuable information.

Abilities Expo
Phone: (800) 385-3085
Outside U.S.A.: (218) 723-9130
Web site: www.abilitiesexpo.com
*Abilities Expo is dedicated to improving the lives of people with disabilities, senior citizens, their families and caregivers as well as educating and supporting healthcare and education professionals. This conference allows one to test new products and services, computers, athletic equipment, mobility products and aids for daily living.

Respite

What is respite? It is a period of rest or relief from the responsibilities for a caregiver. Caring for a child with disabilities 24 hours a day is demanding, energy consuming and requires periodic time off for your own well-being. Parents of children with disabilities need to take regularly scheduled time off by getting away to relax and recharge. This is essential. Don't question whether or not you deserve it, you need it!

Here are some examples of ways to relax and recharge:

1. **Date night.** Find a reliable babysitter that can handle all the special care issues for your child, and go someplace fun or relaxing. Go to dinner (McDonald's or Chateau d'Escargot, who cares, just *Go!*) Go to a movie, or do something interesting at your church or a friend's church.
2. **Exercise.** Go for a walk, bike ride or rollerblading in a nearby park or somewhere safe and have fun!
3. **Reading.** Get out of the house and go to a coffee shop/book store or library.
4. **Music.** Dig out your favorite tapes or CDs and go someplace peaceful, like a park or beach, and listen and let your mind wander.
5. **Prayer.** See chapter 1, Prayer.

Entertainment today does not have to be alcohol, sex/violence–type movies or videos or an expensive restaurant. Ideas for Cheap Dates: Find a bread store that gives out free slices (Montana Mills) and have a coffee or tea and a slice of bread with some old-fashioned conversation, go to the library and peruse the many free magazines and sit together as a couple or if single, enjoy the peace of reading alone.

Call the parks and recreation department and find out about free nature walks at nearby local parks or forest preserves. Ask where there is a wildlife rehabilitation center where they rescue and care for injured animals. Pretend it's 1901. What would your great grandparents do for a relaxing time together? As a couple, sit facing each other on the couch and massage each other's feet, NO TV! Music is OK, so is something good to drink like a warm cup of tea. Intimate conversation and a foot massage is simple old-fashioned fun together. If you are alone, like I (John) was seven years ago as a single parent, rub your own feet!

Overnight and weekend respite services are frequently available to take care of a child with a disability. Check local specialized camps that care for children with disabilities, churches, parks and recreation departments, physical and occupational therapists, and the rehabilitation department at a nearby children's hospital. For more information on finding a camp that serves children with disabilities, see chapter 12, **Recreational Programs**, item 6. *Camps.*

To learn more about respite programs in your area, speak with your child's therapists, healthcare providers and counselors, especially physical and occupational therapists, or contact the children's hospital closest to your home. For example, in the Western New York State and Southern Ontario area, Cradle Beach Camp offers the Weekend Respite Program, Friday 7:00 P.M. to Sunday 3:00 P.M. Parents of children having disabilities are asked the following questions in the Cradle Beach Camp Respite Program brochure:

Do you need time for yourself, to relax and plan activities that you enjoy?
Would the person with a developmental disability living with you enjoy a weekend camping experience?
Have you wished for some free time with other members of your family?
If your response is "Yes" to any of these questions, Cradle Beach Camp Respite may be for you!

For more information on the Cradle Beach Camp Respite Program, contact:

Cradle Beach Camp Respite Program
8038 Old Lakeshore Road
Angola, NY 14006
Phone: (716) 549-0350 or (716) 549-6316
Fax: 716-549-6825
E-mail: PATTYCBC@aol.com
Web site: www.cradlebeach.org

Vacation Planning

In order for the entire family, especially the caregiver(s), to be able to relax and enjoy their vacation, the special needs of the children with a disability must be met. Parents must have confidence that their child is safely cared for with appropriate entertainment and activities, including adequately trained staff. Most resorts are required by law to be handicapped accessible, but you will have more issues that must be addressed before confidently spending money and time away from home.

When you call the resort or vacation site, speak directly to someone in authority, *during business hours*, such as the owner, manager, supervisor of customer service or the director of children's programs. This will avoid missing out on a very special resort or vacation site simply because you receive the wrong information from an uninformed receptionist or desk clerk on duty during the evening hours when you are searching the Web.

Here is the list of questions that consider your child's needs. Have these primary questions written down when you begin calling, sifting through brochures or visiting vacation sites. We suggest you carefully prepare your own list, along with input from all of your child's therapists, healthcare providers and counselors, especially physical and occupational therapists.

Speak with other families of children having the same disabilities as your child. Ask your child's doctor, physical or occupational therapists for names and phone numbers of other families for vacation advice. You will get excellent advice on resorts they would strongly recommend and resorts or vacation sites to avoid.

We found that in order to completely relax, we needed a resort that had a children's program that would meet all the needs of our child and stimulate her to socially interact and have a lot fun becoming independent. Use these questions to tailor-make your vacation, whether it is a full-service resort with a children's program, camping in a nearby state park, going on a cruise or cross-country with a rented camper or RV.

Resort or Vacation Site Questions

1. Are there counselors trained and experienced in caring for children with disabilities?
2. Have these counselors ever cared for a child like ours with these disabilities?
3. What activities, sports and nature things can our child do in your programs?
4. What is the ratio of kids to a counselor?
5. What kind of training or experience do the counselors have?
6. Is there a safe swimming program for our child with these disabilities? Is there a shallow end or separate wading pool and what about steps, easy access handrails, and can children in wheelchairs gain access to the water?
7. If the resort or vacation site doesn't offer these services or is not handicapped accessible, do they know of any nearby resort that does?
8. Where is the closest hospital or nearby pediatrician/family practice physician and the phone numbers? (You may want to get a medical summary typed up from your child's pediatrician or family practice physician in case you need medical care while away. Ask your doctor.)

Don't lose hope! We did find the perfect resort this way, and it was economical! Throughout the long, snowy winters, we enjoy dreaming about how much fun we all had last summer and we look forward to next summer. We even leave extra copies of the resort's brochure and snapshots lying around so we can daydream and look forward to next summer, together as a family.

Here are some organizations with Web sites to help you plan your well-deserved, family vacation:

Access-Able Travel Source, LLC
P O Box 1796
Wheat Ridge, CO 80034
Phone: (303) 232-2979
Fax: (303) 239-8486
E-mail to: bill@access-able.com
Web site: www.access-able.com
* Access-Able Travel Source is dedicated to aiding travelers with disabilities, including adults, with a large database for accessible accommodations and information including scuba diving for persons with all types of disabilities, accessible safaris, sailing, raft trips and sky sailing. They have information on seashore areas that have beach wheelchairs. Click on Travel and Disability Links and Travel Agents and Tour Operators for anyone with special needs.

Medical Travel, Inc.
ADA Vacations Plus Medical Travel
5184 Majorca Club Drive
Boca Raton, Florida 33486 Phone: (800) 778-7953
Fax: (561) 361-9385 E-mail: ada@medicaltravel.org
Web site: www.adavacationsplus.com
*Medical Travel, Inc., is a full-service medical travel agency that caters to patients with medical needs, their families and friends. Their office arranges cruises and land vacations for dialysis patients, patients with respiratory problems, ventilator users and wheelchair users travelers. They advertise they are committed to making travel with medical needs "simple and hassle free."

Emerging Horizons
Web site: www.EmergingHorizons.com
*Newsletter, Emerging Horizons Accessible Travel News

Society for Accessible Travel (SATH)
(formerly called the Society for the Advancement of Travel for the Handicapped)
347 Fifth Ave., Suite 610
New York, NY 10016
Phone: (212) 447-7284
Fax: (212) 725-8253
E-mail: sathtravel@aol.com
Web site: www.sath.org
*The Society for Accessible Travel & Hospitality (SATH) is a nonprofit educational organization that has actively represented travelers with disabilities since 1976. SATH's mission is to promote awareness, respect and accessibility for the disabled.

Trips Inc. Special Adventures
P.O. Box 10885
Eugene, OR 97440
Phone: (800) 686-1013
Fax: (541) 465-9355
E-mail: trips@tripsinc.com
Web site: www.tripsinc.com
* Trips Inc. Special Adventures provides travel outings and vacations to people of various abilities in a safe, respectful and fun atmosphere. Their trips are designed for people with developmental disabilities that require staff assistance for a safe and enjoyable vacation. All of their special adventures are designed to create a stimulating environment that fosters personal and emotional growth, friendship and learning.

Here are some books to help you plan your well-deserved, family vacation:

Fodor's Great American Vacations for Travelers with Disabilities (2nd Edition)
Editors: Donna Cornacchio and Anto Howard
Publisher: Fodors Travel Publishing, Inc., Copyright 1997
ISBN: 0679032258
*This is an excellent travel guide providing travelers and their companions with information on accessibility and other helpful information for travelers with mobility, vision and hearing impairments.

Wheelchair Around the World
Author: Patrick D. Simpson
Publisher: Pentland Press, Copyright 1997
ISBN: 1571970541
*This is a resource guide by an author whose wife is disabled. This guide will teach how to enjoy the world with a disability.

Developing Your Child's Independence

Give your child every opportunity to develop their independence. Your child may not be able to fully dress him/herself, but this should not prevent you from encouraging them in their own capabilities (taking their clothes out of a drawer, finding a place for their shoes, toys, books, etc.).

Don't let guilt and obligation isolate you and your child. Kids want to play and socialize. Join playgroups, or invite children and their parents over to your own home. Able-bodied children are very accepting at a young age and develop close friendships with children having disabilities. Locate those preschool programs that have experience or interest in safely caring for your child's special needs and including them with other able-bodied children. This is known as "mainstreaming." If you need help finding these programs, speak with your child's therapists, healthcare providers and counselors, especially physical and occupational therapists.

Backyard playgrounds can be custom made with numerous handholds, shallower steps and safety railings for your child's enjoyment. This will also draw other children into your backyard, making it easier for your child to have neighborhood friends and fun.

Home tutoring programs can help your child to learn and reason by using books, games and special education computer programs with touch screens, large keyboards, voice-activated computer systems and other assistive technologies. See chapter 5, Assistive Technology Devices and Services.

Schedule free time for your child to do the things that they really enjoy. This could be anything from reading to drawing or calling a friend on the phone. Schedule and protect this free time! It is a common mistake to overload your child with therapy appointments, spending too much time in the car and too many scheduled activities. Children must play to grow. Don't overbook your child!

For more information, see the chapters 9, Toys and chapter 10, Bikes, Wheelchairs, Activity Chairs, Assitance Chairs and Strollers Designed and Adapted for Children with Disabilities. Also see chapter 11, Sports Therapy, chapter 12, Recreational Programs, and chapter 15, Service Dogs.

Looking Out for Your Child's Safety

Parents have a natural instinct to protect their children. This instinct is especially strong if your child has a disability. Medical literature shows that children with disabilities are more susceptible to accidents, physical and even sexual abuse, being hurt by other children (bullies) and being involved with drugs and alcohol. There are many ways that you can prevent these things from happening by teaching your children how to keep themselves safe. By teaching your children safety, you will also help them to become aware of their emotions (i.e., safe, confused, happy, scared, angry and hurt). Help your child identify when these emotions are present by giving them examples. You will also be teaching them how to know what is acceptable, what is not and when to talk to an adult whom they can trust.

Teaching safety to your child is often easier if you include role-playing of different situations and encouraging them to identify what is safe and what is unsafe. It may be a dangerous situation or a situation where they have been hurt, requiring your child to respond by leaving the situation, saying, "No!" telling someone they trust or yelling for help.

Discuss with your child the differences between them being touched appropriately versus inappropriately or harmfully. As an example, appropriate touches would include shaking hands and medical checkups. Inappropriate touches would include someone grabbing your child harshly, pulling their hair or touching their private parts without permission. Teach your child the difference between "good secrets" (a surprise gift or a party) and bad secrets (a grown up who is touching their private parts and they are told not to tell because it is a secret). Instruct your child to tell you or another trusted adult (e.g., teacher) if they are ever told a "bad secret."

As your child approaches puberty, discuss with them the physical changes they will experience. Define the medical names of the body parts but also use more comfortable terms such as "private parts" for genitalia. Failing to discuss the function of a girl's and boy's sexual organs (private parts, genitalia) will increase the risk of sexual abuse, sexually transmitted disease, rape and pregnancy. Teach your children appropriate places to change their clothes (e.g., a girls' or boys' changing room or a bathroom with a door). Inappropriate places would include a classroom where both girls and boys are present, or a bathroom not out of view from others.

Talk to your children about drugs and alcohol. Failure to do so increases their risk of unexpected overdose, drug and alcohol abuse, and becoming corrupted by bad company. Role-play with different examples of how drugs or alcohol could be introduced to your child by either a friend or an adult. Have your child get comfortable with saying "No," leaving the situation or calling home for a ride to get out of trouble.

In order to reinforce these safety issues at home, you must become completely familiar with what your child is learning at school such as the D.A.R.E. (Drugs Abuse Resistance Education) program and other safety programs offered by your local police department.

When you are choosing a personal care provider for your child, make sure you check their background out thoroughly and check their references. Talk to the people they have worked for before and don't be afraid to ask if there have been any abuse, neglect or exploitation issues. Close supervision of the care provider such as a trial run with you staying home or coming back home unexpectedly or early, will give you assurance that your child is safe and in good care. Take the time and effort to develop a close and personal relationship with the care provider to increase trust and their ability to fully care for your child.

Should you have any suspicion of abuse or neglect of your child, be sure to contact Child Protective Services (CPS) and your local police department to report the incident. If your child tells you about an incident in which they were abused, seek out medical care immediately such as going to an emergency room or contacting your child's physician. The physician or nurses will provide support and understanding as well as filing the appropriate paperwork.

It is absolutely necessary for your child's safety, confidence and happiness for you to talk to your child about these personal safety issues. If you decide to avoid talking about these sensitive and critical issues, you may not be protecting your child but actually be placing your child at risk when you are not there to protect them. Good parenting requires teaching our children to be safe when we are not there.

Counseling for Families Facing Challenges

Families with children who have disabilities often face various challenges that result in stress and feelings of guilt, anger, fear, anxiety, sadness and isolation for the parents and the children. This can affect anything from marriage and sibling relationships including sibling rivalry and community relationships (e.g., left out of birthday parties, lack of friends). Often the entire family is affected to some degree and you may want to seek professional counseling so that the family unit stays connected and divorce is avoided. Counseling may be helpful if you have other children in your family and are finding they are having problems at school, difficulties with social interaction with friends, or they are angry or jealous toward the child with special needs.

Where To Go Next

The pastor of your church is a good place to start. Often your pastor can provide you with solid Christian support and encouragement while going through these many challenges. If you or your pastor feels a professional counselor is needed, your pastor can recommend someone to you who has the same Christian values as you.

When you are looking for a professional counselor, make sure the counselor has had experience in working with families with similar disabilities and challenges. Also, make sure the counselor is a licensed professional counselor (LPC) or a nationally certified counselor (NCC). Social workers are another option for counseling services, providing they are licensed. Their licensing requirements vary from state to state. They may have a graduate degree, Master of Social Work (MSW) or the title of "licensed social worker" or "clinical social worker." Additionally, these individuals must be affiliated with their parent professional associations.

Counselors should be affiliated with the American Counseling Association (ACA), psychologists should be affiliated with the American Psychological Association (APA) and social workers are represented by the National Association of Social Work (NASW).

You may be sensitive to seeking professional counseling because feeling weak or defeated; however, counseling may provide you with the support, encouragement and community resources you need to help you through your family challenges. Often family counseling does this by identifying problem areas and providing you with personalized methods to help you. Counseling is successful when you, your family members and the counselor develop a trusting, respectful and empathetic relationship together.

Counseling will not fix family challenges in one visit. It takes time, commitment, trust, respect and patience. If you don't feel comfortable with a counselor after investing a fair and reasonable amount of time, then it is best to find someone you are comfortable with. The decision to seek counseling is a difficult one. Sometimes it is necessary to make the commitment for family counseling for the well-being of the entire family. Pray for God's guidance. There are many counselors who have been successful in enabling families to overcome their challenges in caring for their child with disabilities.

Home and Car Accessibility Issues

Typical home modifications include ramps, railings, hand-holds, wider doors for better wheelchair accessibility, bathroom modifications including grab bars around the toilet and in the tub with a hand-held shower nozzle and tub seat. Chapter 5, Assistive Technology Devices and Services, will provide you with information on home modifications through your local Center for Assistive Technology (CAT) office.

Mini-van and van modifications can include running boards, railings, handholds, automatic doors, ramps and hydraulic lifts for wheelchairs. Contact your local van dealer for a list of local conversion van companies regarding these modifications, which can be very costly. Financial assistance for many of these modifications is available through your local car dealer through:

General Motors through the GM Accessibility Program
Phone: (800) 323-9935
Web site: http://www.GM.com, click on Mobility link

Ford Motor Company, Mobility Motoring Program
Phone: (800) 952-2248, hearing impaired (800) 833-0312
Web site: http://www.ford.com/mobilitymotoring

Maximizing Medical Insurance Reimbursement

Find out which health maintenance organizations (HMOs) or other insurance companies offer the best reimbursement with the least hassle by first speaking to other parents having children with disabilities. Networking with other parents that have solved these insurance reimbursement nightmares is extremely valuable. Next, speak to your child's doctors regarding which HMOs and insurance companies they recommend specific to your child's disabilities.

Next, get to know your child's doctor's insurance person on a first-name basis. Most physicians will have an insurance person dedicated to handling the mountain of insurance reimbursement paperwork required for that doctor's office. This insurance person at your doctor's office usually has a private telephone line. Work closely with this insurance person and they will give you valuable advice on how to fight the HMOs to get reimbursed for not only their office bills, but hospital bills and other products like splints, wheelchairs, orthopedic appliances, orthotics, hospital beds and walkers. Unfortunately, the HMO and insurance company position is to limit spending and reimbursement. The doctor's interest is providing the best possible care for your child. Your child's doctor's insurance person often knows strategies to squeeze the money out of the HMOs and insurance companies, legitimately and fairly. Don't lose hope.

Persistence pays off when dealing with insurance companies. Be as organized as possible with file folders and attend to unpaid bills on a weekly or biweekly basis to keep the pressure on the HMO or insurance companies. If you run into a complete roadblock for legitimate reimbursement, file a grievance directly to the medical director of the HMO or insurance company. This medical director is usually a retired or semi-retired local physician. Unfortunately, the medical director's job includes limiting medical reimbursement. It may help to have your child's doctor proofread your grievance letter prior to your sending it to the medical director. Also, request your child's doctor to send a letter of explanation to justify reimbursement, to accompany your grievance letter. Keep multiple copies of all correspondence in case further help is needed from an attorney, state congressmen or senators. For more information and examples on available legal assistance, see appendix 1, Support Services and Legal Assistance, Western NY State.

Unpaid medical bills are a high source of anxiety for parents of children with disabilities. Stay organized, be persistent and realize it is medically unethical and illegal for a doctor and emergency room or a hospital to refuse caring for your child due to an outstanding bill, or carrying the wrong insurance or no insurance at all. If for any reason, an insurance company drops your coverage or refuses to pay large medical bills, have all correspondence copied and organized for you and your attorney to begin fighting for your child's rights. Regarding other sources of money, grants and donations, contact your local and state organizations supporting your child's medical problems. See chapter 8, Programs and Information Centers in the U.S. and Canada for Persons with Disabilities including SSI (Supplemental Security Income).

Disabilities, Chronic Conditions and Medical Diagnoses in Layperson's Terms

Acquired brain injury (ABI): Brain injury or damage caused by a medical disease.

Amblyopia: Uncorrectable dimness of vision or partial loss of sight.

Amputation: Surgical removal or accidental cutting off of a limb, part of a limb, or a part of the body. AKA is an *above-the-knee* amputation, BKA is *below-the-knee* amputation. Unilateral amputation is one side of the body and bilateral amputation is both sides of the body.

Aphasia: Impaired ability to communicate by speech or writing. Receptive aphasia is the lack of ability to receive or understand words. Expressive aphasia is the lack of ability to express or say words.

Arthritis: Inflammation of a joint. Osteoarthritis (OA) is the most common type of arthritis, also called degenerative joint disease (DJD). OA affects the elderly, but also the disabled with overly stressed joints. OA is made worse by immobilization from prolonged bed rest or being confined in a wheelchair. Juvenile arthritis is a term for any kind of arthritis that affects children, including juvenile rheumatoid arthritis (JRA), lupus, and ankylosing spondylitis.

Asthma: Asthma, also called reactive airway disease, is a chronic lung condition with 1. inflammation (swelling) of the lining of the airways, 2. increased sensitivity to things that trigger the airways to constrict (become smaller) such as allergies, cold, exercise, upper respiratory infection (chest cold), irritants (cigarette smoke, perfume, other strong odors and 3. Obstruction of airflow along with mucus plugging.

Attention deficit and hyperactivity disorder (ADHD): Neurological syndrome with various symptoms including distractibility, short attention span, impulsiveness, hyperactivity and restlessness, which interferes with everyday living.

Autism: Neurological disorder with mild to severe behavioral problems in communicating, responding to the surroundings or interacting with others.

Bipolar disorders: Bipolar refers to the two episodes of manic (frenzied) behavior followed by a major depression (extreme, prolonged sadness/hopelessness) period.

Cerebral palsy (CP): CP is a disorder of body movement, coordination and posture due to a non-progressive injury to the part of the brain called the cerebrum (large area of the brain including the cerebral hemispheres and the basal ganglia). The injury results from very low oxygen (anoxia) occurring before or during birth up to five years of age. The types of CP are *spastic* (very tight, constant muscle contractions), *dyskinetic* (constant, slow writhing movements of mostly the arms, called choreoathetoid movements), *hypotonic* (very weak), and *mixed forms* of CP, which is a combination.

Cerebrovascular accident (CVA): CVA or stroke is a sudden weakness or other neurological symptoms resulting from a blood clot or bleeding in the brain resulting in loss of brain tissue.

Cognitive disability: Brain damage from illness or injury that affects the ability of the person to recognize, judge, sense, reason, understand, or imagine.

Depression: a sinking of the spirits, or dejection, resulting in a lasting, clinical condition.

Developmental disability (DD): Brain damage from illness or injury that interrupts or delays normal growth or development, beginning before the age of 18 months, such as mental retardation/learning disability, cerebral palsy, autism, epilepsy, and Down's syndrome.

Diabetes (DM): Disease of a lack of making enough insulin (DM Type I) or the body does not use insulin properly (DM Type II). Both types result in elevated blood glucose (sugar) levels.

Disability: A medical and legal term signifying loss of function and ability to earn money.

Down's syndrome: Genetic or chromosomal abnormality of chromosome 21 resulting in mild to severe mental retardation/learning disability, along with possibly other birth and physical defects including short neck, large tongue, shortened fingers, joint laxity, oval-shaped eyes, and short height.

Dysarthria: Difficulty in articulation or forming the words due to disease of the central nervous system or problems in speaking due to weakness, poor coordination, or spasm of the muscles around the mouth.

Dyslexia: Condition described by a delay in various areas of learning, such as reading, seen in children of average to above average intelligence.

Epilepsy: Chronic disorder described by sudden attacks of altered brain electrical activity, which can result in a change in the level of consciousness or behavior to generalized convulsions. *Grand mal seizure* is a major convulsion with a loss of consciousness and uncontrolled stiff or jerking body movements. *Petit mal seizure* is a small seizure with a loss of consciousness for a few seconds. *Focal motor seizure* may be a period of confusion, staggering walk, and purposeful movements with facial twitching and garbled speech.

Fetal alcohol syndrome: Disorder found in infants born to alcoholic mothers, which may appear as an infant born with small size and weight, small head size, small eyes and/or small eye openings. There may be delayed brain development and lower intellect, hyperactivity, short attention span, and impulsiveness.

Fragile-X syndrome: Chromosomal abnormality with cognitive and mental impairment, attention deficit, hyperactivity, anxiety, unstable moods, long face, large ears, flat feet, with emotional and behavioral problems.

Friedreich's ataxia: Hereditary disease beginning in childhood, which involves steady, progressive loss of muscle power and coordination due to degeneration of the spinal column and cerebrum (large part of the brain).

Genetic disorders: Conditions resulting from abnormalities in the chromosomes, or genes, which carry the DNA information about the human body in every cell.

Glaucoma: Increased intraocular (inside the eyeball) pressure, which if not treated, may result in poor vision or blindness.

Guillain-Barré syndrome: Neurological syndrome of an unknown cause, but probably due to a virus, resulting in pins-and-needles sensation of the limbs (arms and legs), limb weakness or even complete paralysis.

Hemiparesis: Slight paralysis or partial weakness affecting only one side of the body.

Hemiplegia: Paralysis (complete weakness) affecting only one side of the body.

Huntington's disease: Hereditary brain disease involving progressive degeneration of brain tissue and basal ganglia resulting in sudden, jerky, uncontrollable movements, which are worse with stress or physical exertion.

Hypertension: High blood pressure.

Lability: a sudden change in the emotions without any reason or cause.

Learning disability: Often called a hidden disability, people with learning disabilities often have average to above-average intelligence, with no physical disability. People with learning disabilities have difficulty with getting messages to the brain, making it harder to learn in one or more academic areas. They may not have mental retardation. These people learn to compensate by figuring out on their own or by being taught different ways to learn from the average way other people learn.

Mental retardation (MR): Sub-average general intellectual ability, which is present from the early developmental period of infancy through early childhood. Mental retardation is associated with problems in learning and adjusting socially.

Multiple-sclerosis (MS): Neurological disorder of the brain and spinal cord with many patches of sclerosis (plaques or scarred areas), resulting in weakness, paralysis, trembling hands (tremor), visual problems with controlling eye movement, poor balance, slurred speech and emotional lability (sudden changes). MS occurs in early adult life with flare-ups (exacerbation) and periods of time with lessening or disappearance of symptoms (remission).

Muscular dystrophy (MD): Genetic disease of abnormal muscle, which results in a steady wasting away of the muscle tissue, affecting the muscles under voluntary control and involuntary control.

Myopia: Near-sightedness.

Nystagmus: rapid, jerking-type movements of the eyeballs.

Orthotics: The science of custom making orthopedic appliances (brace/splint) to fit over a certain area of the body, such as the feet, ankle or a back.

Paraplegia: Paralysis or paresis (weakness) of the lower half of the body, the legs.

Paresis: Weakness or incomplete paralysis.

Post-polio syndrome: Syndrome of weakness, paralysis, fatigue, shortness of breath, and balance problems following polio, which is a viral infection of the spinal cord.

Prosthesis: An artificial device, such as an artificial leg or arm.

Quadriplegia: Paralysis or paresis (weakness) of all four limbs both arms and legs.

Scoliosis: Lateral (side-to-side) curvature of the spine.

Seizures: Chronic disorder described by sudden attacks of altered brain electrical activity, which can result in a change in the level of consciousness or behavior to generalized convulsions. See **Epilepsy.**

Spina bifida (SB): A birth defect of an absence of bone in the vertebrae of the spinal column, which allows the spinal cord coverings with sometimes the spinal cord itself to stick out of the back. Scoliosis sometimes occurs, as well.

Spinal cord injury (SCI): Trauma to the spinal cord, which may result in temporary or permanent loss of sensation and movement below the level of injury in the spinal cord. SCI may result in paraplegia or quadriplegia.

Strabismus: Also known as "lazy eye," strabismus results from an imbalance in the eye muscles so both eyes do not look in the same direction.

Syndrome: The signs (seen on exam by the physician) and symptoms (felt by the patient) associated with any illness or injury, which all together, describes the disease.

Traumatic brain injury (TBI): Brain damage from an accident (trauma), which may affect thought, behavior, memory, movement, sensation, and balance. Seizures may result from TBI.

Visual impairment: Disability resulting in reduced or lost vision.

Appendices

We hope these appendices will provide encouragement and suggestions for you to find similar programs in your hometown. In these appendices, we list the support services, legal assistance, sports therapy programs and recreational programs in Western New York State.

- Support Services and Legal Assistance, Western New York State
- Sports Therapy Programs in Western New York State
- Recreational Programs in Western New York State

Appendix A

Support Services and Legal Assistance, Western New York State

Support Services in Western New York State

Erie County Office for the Disabled
95 Franklin Street, Room 626
Buffalo, NY 14202
Phone: (800) 662-1220
(716) 858-6215
*The Erie County Office of the Disabled was created to ensure that Erie County's citizens with disabilities would have a direct voice in county government; to make available to such citizens an advocate who could work within the county structure to develop and enhance services; and to oversee facilities and programs by the county.

Family Support Services
Western New York Developmental Disabilities Services Office (DDSO)
For Allegany, Cattaraugus, & Chautauqua Counties: (800) 292-5735
For Erie, Genesee, Niagara, & Orleans Counties: (800) 487-6310, ext. 2151
*Provides help, direction, training, answers to questions, time for you to get away and take a break (called respite). Programs offered include Family Empowerment, Medicaid Waiver Programs, Case Management and Early Intervention, Counseling, Advocacy Services, Parent Support Groups, Family Member Training and Behavior Intervention Programs and Crisis Intervention.

Great Lakes Orthopedic Labs, Inc.
219 Bryant Street
Buffalo, NY 14202
Phone: (716) 878-7307
*Provides custom made orthopedic braces and artificial limbs for all ages.

The Robert Warner Rehabilitation Center of
The Children's Hospital of Buffalo
Pediatric Rehabilitation Services
Kaleida Health
936 Delaware Avenue
Buffalo, NY 14209
Phone: (716) 878-7557
Fax: (716) 888-3834
*Providing comprehensive rehabilitation services consisting of diagnostic, evaluative, and therapeutic services to children in Western New York and surrounding areas with know or suspected disabilities. Each clinic or program is comprised of an interdisciplinary team of specialists specifically selected to meet your child's needs. The whole child is our primary focus of care. Services are family focused and provided in conjunction with pediatricians and community resources.

Legal Assistance in Western New York State

Bouvier O'Connor Attorneys at Law
Bruce Goldstein, Esq.
350 Main Street, Suite 1400
Buffalo, NY 14202
Phone: (716) 856-1344
Fax: (716) 856-1369
Web site: www.bouvierlaw.com

Legal Aid Bureau of Buffalo, Inc
237 Main Street, Suite 1602
Buffalo, NY 14203-2723
Phone: (716) 853-9555

NYS Education Department
Special Education Training & Resource Center (SETRC)
1 Commerce Plaza
Albany, NY 12234
Phone: (800) 344-9611

Neighborhood Legal Services, Inc.
Handicapped Rights Unit
295 Main St., Ellicott Square, Room 495
Buffalo, NY 14203
Phone: (716) 847-0650
Fax: (716) 847-0227
Web site: www.adickerson@nls.org

State University of New York at Buffalo
Legal Assistance Program
P.O. Box 9
Getzville, NY 14068-0009
Phone: (716) 645-2167
Fax: (716) 645-2900

Support Services in Western New York State

Agape Parents' Fellowship, Inc.
P.O. Box 2205
Blasdell, NY 14219
Phone: (716) 827-5407

Association for Retarded Children
470 Franklin Street
Buffalo, NY 14202
Phone: (716) 886-3166

Child & Adolescent Psychiatric Clinic
3350 Main Street
Buffalo, NY 14214
Phone: (716) 835-4011

Child Behavior Associates
Kathleen O'Mara, M.S., Director
64 Wood Acres Avenue
East Amherst, NY 14051
Phone: (716) 689-7351

Children's Hospital
Department of Child Psychiatry
& Behavioral Sciences
219 Bryant Street
Buffalo, NY 14222
Phone: (716) 878-7609

Erie 2 Chataqua-Cataraugus BOCES
9520 Fredonia Stockton Road
Fredonia, NY 14063
Phone: (800) 344-9611
(716) 672-4371

Mental Health Association of Erie County
1237 Delaware Avenue
Buffalo, NY 14209
Phone: (716) 886-1424

Parent Network Center
250 Delaware Avenue, Suite 3
Buffalo, New York 14202
Phone: (716) 853-1570

Robert Warner Rehabilitation Center
936 Delaware Avenue
Buyffalo, NY 14209
Phone: (716) 883-5810

State University of Buffalo
Psychology Clinic
4230 Ridge Lea Road
Buffalo, NY 14226
Phone: (716) 831-3067

SUNYAB Reading Education Clinic
Baldy Hall
Amherst Campus
Buffalo, NY 14260
Phone: (716) 636-2491

Tonawanda Community Counseling Center
36 Delaware Avenue
Tonawanda, NY 14150
Phone: (716) 693-4622

United Cerebral Palsy of Western New York, Inc.
7 Community Drive
Cheektowaga, NY 14225
Phone: (716) 505-5500

WNY Association for Learning Disabled
2555 Elmwood Avenue
Kenmore, NY 14217
Phone: (716) 874-7200
Fax: (716) 874-7205
Web site: www.ldaofwny@aol.com

Youth Advocacy Program
775 Main Street
Suite 319
Buffalo, NY 14203
Phone: (716) 853-0600
Fax: (716) 853-0605

Appendix B
Sports Therapy Programs,
Western New York State

- Adaptive Downhill Skiing Therapy
- Aquatic Therapy (Swimming Therapy)
- Dance Therapy
- Horseback Riding Therapy
- Skating Therapy

Adaptive Downhill Skiing Therapy Programs in Western NY State

Holiday Valley Resort
Bill Lounsbury Adaptive Ski Program
P.O. Box 370
Ellicottville, NY 14731
Phone: (716) 699-2345
Contact: Doug Braun, Program Director
Phone: (716) 699-2345, ext. 4051

Program Description: The Lounsbury Adaptive Ski Program accommodates individuals 6 years and over with most challenges and disabilities including amputees, post-polio, cerebral palsy, spina bifida, traumatic head injury, multiple sclerosis, blind/visually impaired, mental disabilities, spinal cord injuries and other conditions requiring a wheel chair. Specialized adaptive skiing techniques and equipment are used to accommodate most disabilities and challenges. The staff consists of instructors from the Holiday Valley Ski School and 35 dedicated volunteers offering close to one-on-one instruction. Training follows the Professional Ski Instructors of America's (PSIA) American Teaching System (ATS) and the Adaptive Instruction of PSIA and Disabled Sports/USA (DSUSA) to ensure safety. The skier's experience may offer a positive effect on developing independence, self-confidence, self-motivation, increased physical strength and coordination, peer interaction and improved self-image, which carries over to other activities of daily life.

Lessons: Lessons are 2 hours, by appointment, 7 days a week at 10:00 a.m. and 1:00 p.m.

Cost: $25.00/ 2-hour lesson with ski and adaptive equipment and lift ticket included. Book of four lessons, with ski equipment and lifts, is $80.00.

Directions: Approximately 60 minutes south of the City of Buffalo. Route 219, South, to Springville, NY and proceeding on route 219 to Ellicottville, NY.

Appendix B

HoliMont Ski Resort
The Phoenix Group Adaptive Ski Program
Route 242 Fish Hill Road
P.O. Box 279
Ellicottville, NY 14731
Phone: (716) 699-2320, Slope Report (716) 699-4720
Fax: (716) 699-5029
E-Mail: www.holimont.com
Phone: (716) 699-8159, HoliMont Snow Sports Center (Ski School)
Contact: Chuck Richardson, Program Director
Program Description: The Phoenix Adaptive Ski Program accommodates individuals with most challenges and disabilities including amputees, autism, post-polio, cerebral palsy, spina bifida, traumatic head injury, multiple sclerosis, blind/visually impaired, mental disabilities, seizure disorder and spinal cord injuries. Specialized adaptive skiing techniques and equipment are used to accommodate most challenges and disabilities. The staff consists of instructors from the HoliMont Snow Sports Center and many dedicated volunteers offering close to one-on-one instruction. Training follows the Professional Ski Instructors of America's (PSIA) American Teaching System (ATS) and the Adaptive Instruction of PSIA to ensure safety. The skier's experience may offer a positive effect on developing independence, self-confidence, self-motivation, increased physical strength and coordination, peer interaction and improved self-image, which carries over to other everyday life activities.

Lessons: Lessons are by appointment. Monday-Friday, HoliMont is open to the public. On Saturday and Sunday, HoliMont Ski Resort is only open to HoliMont members. Lessons are 2 hours during the weekday for the public and on weekends for HoliMont members and member's guests.

Cost: $300.00 per student for the ski season. Rental equipment, including helmets, is also available. Contact the Snow Sports Center, 699-8159.

Directions: Approximately 60 minutes south of the City of Buffalo. Route 219, South, to Springville, NY and proceeding on route 219 to Ellicottville, NY. Go through town, through the stoplight, continuing on Route 242, South, and approximately one more mile to the entrance to HoliMont.

191

Kissing Bridge Ski Resort
Adaptive Ski Program
Route 240
Glenwood, NY 14069
Phone: (716) 592-4963
Contact: Nancy Maressa, Program Director (716) 648-6895
Program Description: The Adaptive Ski Program accommodates various challenges and disabilities including: amputees, autism, birth defects, brain injuries, cerebral palsy, developmentally disabled, learning disabled, multiple sclerosis, post-accident, post-polio, stroke and visually impaired/blind. This program serves ambulatory (walking) children and adults primarily on Saturday. Non-ambulatory (non-walking) children and adults are referred to the Lounsbury Adaptive Ski Program at Holiday Valley Ski Resort, Ellicottville, NY. Weekday group skiing sessions are available by contacting Kissing Bridge Ski Resort in advance to make specific arrangements. Specialized adaptive skiing techniques and equipment are used to accommodate most challenges and disabilities. The adaptive skiing experience may offer a positive effect on developing independence, self-confidence, self-motivation, increased physical strength and coordination, peer interaction and improved self-image, which carries over to other activities of daily life.

Lessons: Adaptive ski lessons are held on Saturdays, beginning the second week in January, and run for 6 weeks. One-hour lessons are at 1:30 PM and 2:30 PM and are by appointment only. The student/teacher ratio is close to one-on-one with the staff having many volunteers and instructors. The instructors and volunteers try to put the students into a group environment at the first opportunity. The goal of the Kissing Bridge Adaptive Ski Program is to encourage participants into the skiing mainstream by providing them with lifetime recreational capability.

Cost: $65.00/ six, one-hour lessons, including lift tickets. $50.00 for rental equipment for six ski lessons. Sign up at North Ski Area, inside ticket center, at the counter.

Directions: Approximately 30-45 minutes south of the City of Buffalo. Route 219, South, exit onto Armor Duells Road, and follow "Kissing Bridge" signs to Route 240, South.

Peek'n Peak Ski Resort
Adaptive Downhill Ski Program
1405 Olde Road
P.O. Box 360
Findley Lake, NY 14736
Phone: (716) 355-4141, extension 7350 or 7364
Contact: Don Haringa
E-mail: www.info@pknpk.com
Web site: www.pknpk.com
Program Description: The Peek'n Peak Adaptive Ski Program accommodates individuals with most challenges and disabilities in downhill and cross-country skiing and also snowshoeing.

Lessons: Lessons are by appointment. The director, Don Haringa, individually determines the needs of the skier and then selects the specific adaptive ski instructor, certified with the Professional Ski Instructor of America (PSIA).

Cost: $10.00/ 1-hour lesson with adaptive equipment (outriggers, edgy-wedgies) at no expense.

Directions: From Buffalo, NY, travel west on I-90 to Route 17, (Exit 10A). From Route 17, Exit at Findley Lake (Exit 4). Turn south on Route 426 and follow the signs to the resort area; Approximately 5 miles.

Aquatic Therapy (Swimming Therapy) Programs in Western New York State

Aquatic Therapy Program

Suburban Spine and Rehab
115 Flint Road
Williamsville, NY 14221
Phone: (716) 632-5600

Program Description: Physical and occupational therapists through Children's Hospital of Buffalo/Kaleida Health, Occupational and Physical Therapy Department conduct aquatic therapy. Children and young adults ages 0 – 21 with cerebral palsy, developmental disabilities, juvenile rheumatoid arthritis (JRA) and orthopedic injuries receive aquatic therapy in a warm water (92 – 94°F), therapy pool. Sessions are 30 minutes long, offered up to four days a week in 10-week sessions. Most medical insurance policies are accepted along with private payment. Contact Physical/Occupational Therapy at (716) 878-7470 for 3-21 year olds and Early Intervention Program at (716) 878-7640 for 0-3 year olds and for parent/infant group sessions.

Ken Kurtz, Physical Therapy and Associates

8705 Sheridan Dr.
Williamsville, NY 14221
Phone: (716) 631-1212

Program Description: One-on-one aquatic therapy such as range of motion and stretching is directed by a physical therapist in a specially designed pool, with warm water (90 - 92°F). Most medical insurance policies are accepted along with private payment. Chris Merk, Physical Therapy Assistant, is the person to contact as the pool director.

Aquatic Therapy Program of Batavia

Western New York Physical and Occupational Therapy Group
Batavia Office
United Memorial Medical Center, Cary Hall
16 Bank Street
Batavia, NY 14020
Phone: (716) 343-3131, extension 298

Program Description: Physical and occupational therapists direct individual-ized aquatic therapy with both exercise and treatment. Aquatic therapy is conducted in warm water (88° – 90°F) at the near-by YMCA in Batavia with entrances on both Bank and Main Streets. Most medical insurance policies are accepted along with private payment.

Aquatic Therapy Program of Lockport

Western New York Physical and Occupational Therapy Group
Lockport Office
5875 South Transit Road
Lockport, NY 14094
Phone: (716) 433-9058
Program Description: Physical and occupational therapists direct individual-
ized aquatic therapy with both exercise and treatment. Aquatic therapy is
conducted in warm water (88° – 90°F) at the near-by YMCA in Lockport on
East Avenue. Most medical insurance policies are accepted along with private
payment.

Arthritis Foundation Aquatic Program

Western New York Physical and Occupational Therapy Group, PLLC
Weinberg Campus, Outpatient
2700 North Forest Road
Getzville, NY 14068
Phone: (716) 639- 3330, extension 475 or 409
Program Description: Patients with arthritis and neurological disorders
including cerebral palsy receive aquatic therapy in a shallow (4 foot), warm
water (92°F) pool, that is wheelchair accessible. Most medical insurance poli-
cies are accepted along with private payment. The persons to contact are
Shirley Barberic, Physical Therapy Assistant and David Wojtowicz, Physical
Therapist.

Athleticare Physical Therapy

Mercy Ambulatory Care Center
3669 Southwestern Blvd.
Orchard Park, NY 14127
Phone: (716) 828-2455
Program Description: Under controlled conditions of a therapy pool with
warm water (92 - 94°F), a physical therapist conducts aquatic therapy for
children and adults. Ambulatory patients are preferred. Most medical insurance policies are accepted along with private payment. Person to contact is
Tim Bean, Physical Therapist Assistant.

Baker Victory Services, Aquatic Therapy Program
180 Martin Road
Lackawanna, NY 14218
Phone: (716) 828-9325
Program Description: Baker Victory Services conducts an aquatic therapy program in Early Intervention called "Water Play," for ages 1 – 3 years. The warm water (92°F) pool is 4 feet deep. Aquatic therapy is held on Saturdays: 10:00 a.m. – 10:45 a.m. and 10:45 a.m. – 11:30 p.m. and also on Tuesdays: 6:00 p.m. – 6:45 p.m. and 6:45 – 7:30 p.m. for 6-week sessions. If a child is identified by the school district's department of special education as requiring early intervention, then these services are added to the Individualized Family Service Plan (IFSP), and there is no cost. The contact person is Anita Berger, Ongoing Service Coordinator.

Curtis DuBois and Associates Physical Therapy, Aquatic Therapy Program
Woodstream Professional Park
2111 Sawyer Drive
Niagara Falls, NY 14304
(In Wheatfield, across from Summit Park Mall)
Pone: (716) 731-2195
Program Description: Aquatic therapy is conducted in a wheelchair-accessible, warm-water (92 – 95°F) pool that has a Hoyer lift. All children are welcome, especially children ages 0 – 3 years in the Early Intervention program as designated on the child's IEP. Most medical insurance policies are accepted along with private payment. Persons to contact are Jill Bosco, Physical Therapist and Rebecca Dena, Physical Therapist.

Erie-2-Chautauqua-Cattraugus Board of Cooperative Educational Services (BOCES-2), Aquatic Therapy Program

Baker Road Education Center
3340 Baker Road
Orchard Park, NY 14127
Phone: (716) 662-0135

Program Description: Children that receive special education services within the Erie-2-Chautauqua-Cattraugus Board of Cooperative Educational Services (BOCES-2) may be eligible for this aquatic therapy program. Each student must have been screened and recommended by their BOCES-2 Physical Therapist. Adaptive Physical Education (APE) Instructors and recreation therapists administer the aquatic therapy program.

The pool is a specially designed, wheelchair-accessible, warm-water (86° – 88°F) pool, called the "Happiness Pool." It is located at the Western New York Developmental Disabilities Services Office (formerly called West Seneca Developmental Center), Building #9, 1200 East and West Road, West Seneca, NY 14224; Telephone: (716) 674-6300, extension 3825, Michelle Saffire, Recreational Therapist and Day Care Coordinator. Sessions are approximately one hour with one-on-one supervision. There are approximately 15 children per session, 2-3 sessions per week. Cost is covered by BOCES-2 as part of the child's school-based special education therapy program. The BOCES-2 Aquatic Therapy Program is conducted throughout the school year. Danielle O'Connor, the Supervisor of Instructional Programs for BOCES-2, is the person to contact at 662-0135.

New York State School for the Blind, Aquatic Therapy Program

2A Richmond Avenue
Batavia, NY 14020
Phone: (716) 343-5384, option 1, then extension 205

Program Description: Adaptive Physical Education (APE) Instructors and other supervisory personnel conduct aquatic therapy in a specially designed, warm-water pool, which can automatically adjust the depth for the specific needs of the patient. Aquatic therapy is done during the day and select evenings for clients of the New York State School for the Blind and those living in the Western New York. The person to contact is Jennifer Spas Ervin, Superintendent.

Dance Therapy Programs in Western New York State

Dance Special Inc.
Nonprofit organization
16 Sunnyside Place
Buffalo, NY 14207-2237
Phone: (716) 873-0593
Program Description: Offering a modified dance program designed to accommodate children and adults that are mentally and/or physically challenged.

Moves-N-Motions
5820 Seneca Street
Elma, NY 14059
Phone: (716) 675-0319
Program Description: By combining music and dance instruction, dance therapy provides the student cognitive, emotional, social and physical development to both ambulatory and non-ambulatory children.

Moving Miracles, Inc. Dance Program
327 Empourium Ave.
West Seneca, NY 14224
Phone/FAX: (716) 656-1321
Web site: http://www.west.net/~jazz/miracles
Program Description: Moving Miracles, Inc. is a dance/movement program for children, adolescents and adults who are exceptionally challenged; mentally, physically and/or emotionally. Many of the "Moving Miracles" have a form of cerebral palsy and are afflicted with complex seizure disorders as well. Autism, developmental delays, Down's syndrome, attention deficit and hyperactivity disorder and behavioral challenges are obstacles that Moving Miracles, as a dance company, have been victoriously dancing with everyday.

Horseback Riding Therapy Programs in Western New York State

Buffalo Therapeutic Riding Center
(Buffalo Equestrian Center)
950 Amherst Street
Buffalo, NY 14216
Phone: (716) 877-9295

Centaur Stride Therapeutic Riding, Inc.
Jones Road, P.O. Box 174
Westfield, NY 14787
Phone: (716) 326-4318
Contact: Claudia Monroe, P.T.

Equistar Therapeutic Horseback Riding
Miriam Smith, Executive Director
3148 Hess Road
Appleton, NY 14008
Phone: (716) 433-8816

High Hurdles Therapeutic Riding
Judy Feine, Instructor
P.O. Box 526
Sardinia, NY 14134
Phone: (716) 496-5551
E-mail: sasiequine@juno.com

Lothlorien Therapeutic Horseback Riding
15 Reiter Road
East Aurora, NY 14052
Phone: (716) 655-1335
Contact: Carol Knauer, Program Director

Skating Therapy Programs in Western New York State
Skating Association for the Blind and Handicapped (SABAH), Inc.
1200 East & West Road
West Seneca, NY 14224
Phone: (716) 675-SABA (7222)
Fax: (716) 675-7223
E-mail: sabah@sabahinc.org
Web site: www.sabahinc.org
Program Description: By using special equipment such as adapted walkers
and skates designed to fit over ankle braces, children and adults learn how to
enjoy the freedom and self-expression of ice skating with some assistance
from dedicated, trained volunteers and skating instructors. SABAH provides
ice- skating therapy throughout various ice-skating arenas in Western NY
State.

Sled Hockey (also called Sledge Hockey in Canada)

U.S. Sled Hockey
Niagara Challengers
Rich DeGlopper
P.O. Box 235
Amherst, NY 14226
Phone: (716) 874-7411, ext. 7327 ; (716) 875-4864 (Gail Balsdon)
Program Description: Sled Hockey is an alternative winter sport that uses the rules of hockey. The skaters sit on a specially designed sled and use two short ice picks to propel themselves across the ice. Standard hockey rules apply including legal body contact and slap shots.

Appendix C
Recreational Programs, Western New York State

- Baseball
- Boys and Girls Clubs
- Camps
- Empire State Games
- Guild for Children with Special Needs
- Parks and Recreation Departments
- Sailing
- Soccer
- Special Olympics

Baseball Programs in Western New York State

Program Description: All of these baseball programs run from May to July. Rules and playing conditions are adapted to fit any disability. For more information, contact the people listed below, or Mr. Ron Hoeltke, (716) 695-5333.

Hamburg, NY Challenger Baseball
Person to contact: Mike King, (716) 648-1495 or Tim Holscher, (716) 649-1697

LaSalle Little League of Niagara Falls, NY
Person to contact: Don Pitlik, (716) 773-3427

Pendleton, NY Challenger Baseball for Pendleton and Lockport, NY
Person to contact: Cathy Patterson, (716) 434-9427

Tonawanda, NY American Little League
Person to contact: Ron Hoeltke, (716) 695-5333

Boys and Girls Club

Boys and Girls Club of the Tonawanda's
Program Description: Outdoor Soccer is held September and October. Indoor Soccer is held October through December. Basketball is held January through March. The Boys and Girls Club of the Tonawanda's is also available for children in the special challenger programs for other activities. Person to contact: Bob Obracta, (716) 695-7887 (home) or 693-2307 (club).

Camps

Camps in the Northeast United States
For the Easter Seals Camps in the Northeast Region, including overnight camps in New Hampshire and Connecticut, day camps in New York State and both overnight/day Camps in New Jersey, contact Mr. Doug Gordon, phone: (603) 621-3601.

Camps in Western New York State
Cradle Beach Camp Respite Program
8038 Old Lakeshore Road
Angola, NY 14006
Phone: (716) 549-0350 or (716) 549-6316
Fax: 716-549-6825
E-mail: PATTYCBC@aol.com
Web site: www.cradlebeach.org
*Cradle Beach offers recreational services to disabled children ages 9-16. Cradle Beach is a 10-day residual camp setting. Registered nurses and a 24-hour infirmary are on site.

Empire State Games

Empire State Games for the Physically Challenged
SUNY Brockport
Brockport, New York
Phone: (716) 395-5620
TTY: (631) 669-8464
Program Description: The Empire State Games for the Physically Challenged is a free program of competition and fitness workshops for young people with physical disabilities. The goals of the Empire State Games is to provide a program in which physically challenged children can be introduced to sports competition and fitness in an environment, safe to themselves and their fellow competitors, which is adapted to their unique needs and abilities. The Games for the Physically Challenged are open to all children ages 5 through 21 who are amputees, blind or visually impaired, deaf or hearing impaired, spinal cord injured, have cerebral palsy or other disabilities. The Empire State Games are a program of the New York State Office of Parks, Recreation and Historic Preservation.

Guild for Children with Special Needs

Program Description: Bowling is held every other Saturday, October through March. The Guild also has many other programs available for children in special education such as arts and crafts. Person to contact: Linda Becker, (716) 694-4885.

Parks and Recreation Departments of Western New York State

Cattaraugus County, City of Olean Parks and Recreation
Phone: (716) 376-5666

Chattacqua County, Department of Public Facilities, Parks Division
Phone: (716) 661-8400

Erie County Parks and Recreation
Phone: (716) 858-8355, Recreation Division

Niagara Frontier State Parks and Recreation Region
Phone: (716) 278-1770

Sailing Programs in Western New York State

Sailing Program for People with Disabilities
Through the Buffalo Community Boating Center
Small Boat Harbor
901 Fuhrmann Boulevard
Buffalo, NY 14203
Phone: (716) 842-1276, 849-1174
Program Description: The Buffalo Community Boating Center **Sailing Program for People with Disabilities** allows novices and sailors alike to sail without compromise alongside non-disabled and less-disabled peers.

Seven Seas Sailing
284 Furhman Blvd @ RCR Skyway Marina
Buffalo, NY 14203
Phone: (716) 824-1505
Email: www.SevenSeasSailing.com
Program Description: **Seven Seas Sailing** is developing a program for individuals with special needs including Multiple Sclerosis, Cerebral Palsy and other disabilities to enjoy sailing. Executive Director is Bill Zimmerman and the Senior Instructor is Gibb Bradbury, CAPT, USCG, who is a certified Instructor with the American Sailing Association (ASA) School and the U.S. Sail School.

Soccer Programs in Western New York State

Soccer, Outdoor/Indoor
Person to contact: Ron Hoeltke, (716) 695-5333

Questionnaire

We need each other's help.

The best source of reliable information is another experienced parent of a child with disabilities. We call it "networking." Write to us and share what you have learned. Also let us know of any new and useful information. Please also let us know of any error or anything we left out in our handbook along with your detailed corrections and suggestions. If you are, for example, a physician, therapist, educator, manufacturer, administrator, volunteer, etc., please let us know about any new services, products or advice you can offer to help parents of children with disabilities. Along with your question, suggestion, service or product, please include your full mailing address, phone numbers, fax, e-mail and Web site addresses and if we have your permission to reproduce your information in our next handbook. Attach extra pages if necessary. Thank you for mailing us your contributions. We will review all questionnaires and evaluate all the information for possible inclusion in the next edition of the *Handbook for Parents of Children with Disabilities*.

John and Janice Sterba
P.O. Box 842
East Aurora, NY 14052-0842

Questionnaire

The Complete Handbook for
Parents with Disabled Children
Order Form

Book Price: $19.99, U.S. Dollars

Individual Books, order from*:*

ACW Press
5501 N. 7th. Ave. #502
Phoenix, AZ 85013
(800) 931-BOOK
or contact your local bookstore

Shipping from ACW Press: $3.00 for the first book and $1.00 for each additional book (US, Canada, Mexico) and for International orders, $6.00 for the first book and $2.00 for each additional book.

Bulk-Order Books, order by mail, using only a check or money order payable to, "John and Janice Sterba" (sorry, no credit cards accepted). Send your check and completed order form to:

John and Janice Sterba
Box 842
East Aurora, NY 14052-2233

Please send *The Complete Handbook for Parents with Disabled Children* **to:**

Name: _____

Address: _____(P.O. Box not accepted)

City: _____ State: _____

Zip: _____   Telephone: (_____) _____

E-mail Address: _____

	Quantity	Total Price
Unit Price, $19.99 (U.S.)		
*For New York State Residents, Please Add Appropriate Sales Tax: New York State County: Sales Tax %:		
Shipping & Handling:		

# of Books	U.S. (Lower 48)	U.S. (Alaska/Hawaii)	Canada
2–5	$15.25	$39.50	$23.25
6–10	$16.25	$46.50	$27.25
11–20	$20.25	$60.50	$33.25
21–30	$25.25	$71.75	$41.50
31–40	$29.25	$83.75	$47.50

For over 40 Books, please use multiples of the above scale.
For International Orders, please write to us and include your E-mail address and we will calculate 2nd Day-Air Shipping and Handling cost.

Total Amount Due: